ARCHIVAL APPRAISAL

by
FRANK BOLES
in association with
Julia Marks Young

Neal-Schuman Publishers, Inc.
New York   London

Published by Neal-Schuman Publishers, Inc.
100 Varick Street
New York, NY 10013

Printed and bound in the United States of America.

This book is printed on acid-free paper which meets the standard
established by the American National Standard Institute Committee
for Information Science—-Permanence of Paper for Printed Library
Materials. (Z–39–48, 1984.)

Library of Congress Cataloging-in-Publication Data

Boles, Frank.
   Archival appraisal / by Frank Boles in association with Julia
Marks Young.
      p.   cm.
   Includes bibliographical references and index.
   ISBN 1-55570-064-0
   1. Archival materials--Valuation.   I. Young, Julia Marks.
II. Title.
CD971.B58   1991
025.2'814--dc20
                                     91-25102
                                        CIP

Contents

List of Figures

v

List of Tables

Preface

Archival Appraisal was written to increase the understanding of how archivists select records for long-term storage. The goals here are twofold. First, *Archival Appraisal* is intended to improve the practice of selection among archivists by creating a better understanding of the methodology underlying selection. Second, it is intended as a means to share the archival selection methodology with other information professionals who may find the archival paradigm, in whole or in part, applicable to other areas of information management where selection is important.

In 1983 an unexpected piece of good fortune began the chain of events leading to *Archival Appraisal.* The University of Michigan's Bentley Historical Library was awarded a large grant from the Andrew J. Mellon Foundation to fund an ongoing fellowship program in archival research. Harold Shapiro, then president of the University, dropped by the Mellon Foundation's New York office the day after the grant to the Bentley Library was announced. An officer of the Foundation expressed a willingness to fund similar projects in archival research. President Shapiro mentioned that "a little money" could be profitably spent on dealing with university's own records, and to the surprise of all concerned, the Mellon Foundation added "a little money" for that purpose to the previously announced grant.

The University Archives and Records Program staff, consisting of Julia Marks Young and myself, were given a free hand to determine how to spend this windfall. We decided that the most pressing problem facing us was rationalizing the appraisal of university records. Although formally trained as archivists, neither of us was satisfied with the way university documentation decisions were made. Too many times records were kept because someone said they were "good stuff" without any rigorous analysis underlying that vague phrase. The goal of our project was to determine just what we, as archivists, meant when we declared specific records to be "good stuff."

Over the course of two summers we examined the literature on appraisal, debated its merits both between ourselves and with the Bentley Library Fellows, and slowly began to rationalize the elements of appraisal. Our thoughts on the matter were ultimately published in a jointly authored article, "Exploring the Black Box: The Appraisal of University Administrative Records."

Although the complicated "wiring diagrams" of appraisal elements described in the "Black Box" article seemed sensible in theory, we could not demonstrate their widespread applicability. Indeed, our review of the archival literature verified that there was almost no objective research supporting appraisal criteria. We began to consider how we could "field test" our ideas and, again with the assistance of Mellon Foundation funds distributed through the Bentley Library, we developed a testing method using a numerical ranking system and found a few archivists willing to test applying it.

The success of this initial test led us to seek grant funding to underwrite a larger study. Financial support was made available through the National Historical Publications and Records Commission, and our colleagues throughout the country were extremely cooperative in testing out theories about appraisal. The two-year project led directly to the data and conclusions published here.

As it turned out, the way archivists select material for long-term retention was more complex than we had initially imagined. Many of the familiar bromides of the appraisal literature proved difficult to define, or inapplicable in practice. The process of appraisal, we discovered, is one that gives up its secrets grudgingly. Although this book unravels some of appraisal's mysteries, it leaves many more questions to be explored. *Archival Appraisal* should not be read as a definitive study. It is intended to be part of a continuing professional dialogue through which will come a better understanding of how to select records for retention.

The professional debts we have incurred in the years during which this project has been underway are almost too numerous to list. *Archival Appraisal* benefitted enormously from the thought, comments, and writings of many individuals, and from generous financial support.

We must first thank the Andrew J. Mellon Foundation for the special grant to the Bentley Historical Library that supported the initial research. We are also grateful to the National Historical Publications and Records Commission for a major grant which made possible the research that forms the core of the study upon which this book is based.

We are further indebted to the many archivists who participated in the various phases of this study. Working in institutions across the

United States, they gave unselfishly of their time and their ideas in an effort to improve the quality of the research. Although sometimes what they said was not what we wanted to hear, it was almost always what we needed to hear. The contributions of those who cooperated in the work were enormous, and their influence can be seen on almost every page. Although it is impossible to thank each by name, we should particularly like to acknowledge the assistance of: Elizabeth Adkins, Bob Bailey, Tracey Berezansky, Ann Bowers, Paul Chestnut, John Daly, Susan Davis, Paul Ericksen, James Folts, Tom Frusciano, Forrest Galey, Ed Galvin, June Lannae Graham, Larry Hackman, Margaret Hedstrom, H.T. Holmes, Alan Kolowitz, Joan Krizack, Kevin Leonard, Dan Lorello, William Maher, Avra Michelson, Fredric Miller, Tom Mills, Jim O'Toole, Charles Palm, Patrick Quinn, Helen Samuels, Robert Shuster, Robert Sink, Deborah Skaggs, Cynthia Swank, Terri Thompson, George Tselos, Anne Van Camp, Donna Webber, Tom Wilsted, Joel Wurl, and Paul Yon.

We are also indebted to our colleagues at the Bentley Historical Library who contributed to this volume in many ways. Francis X. Blouin, Jr., Thomas E. Powers, and William K. Wallach, in particular, have aided and facilitated this work and we are thankful to each for their assistance.

My deepest intellectual debt is to Julia Marks Young. Throughout the research and early drafts of this volume, Julia's ideas, comments, and sharp editorial pen provided a valuable counterpoint to my own ideas, comments, and tendency to reinvent the English language in uncongenial ways. For a number of reasons she was unable to see the volume through to its conclusion, a fact I much regret. In the last stages of editing I was assisted by Patricia Rogers, who took over Julia's blue pen and much improved the book with tactfully suggested editorial changes.

Finally, and most important, I must acknowledge the assistance of my wife, Valerie. Over the past several years she has heard and read more about appraisal than any nonarchivist needs, or wants, to hear and see. She has borne all this with good grace and has often suggested direct ways to cut to the heart of complex ideas. I am grateful for her intellectual clarity, as well as her patience.

Frank Boles
Ann Arbor, Michigan

1

An Overview

The selection of records for archival retention is the most basic archival activity. Archivists have no graver responsibility than deciding what information they will preserve for society. Although many different information specialists make decisions about the kinds of information available in a particular place and the manner in which that information is organized, archivists bear the unique responsibility of deciding if the information itself will be preserved. An archivist who destroys records does so with the assumption that the information within those documents will be lost forever. There is no interlibrary loan system that can locate another copy, no microfilm stored in an underground vault that can be used instead of the original, no backup computer tape that can be mounted on a tape drive and read. Unlike decisions made by other information specialists, an archivist's appraisal decision is usually final and irrevocable.

To learn how archivists arrive at their decisions, a study funded by the National Historical Publications and Records Commission (NHPRC) was designed to appraise archival practice at 15 institutions. The results of the study were supplemented by an examination of relevant secondary literature in the fields of archives, librarianship, and decision making. As a result of what was learned from both the study and the literature, this book is organized around several themes and questions. Before discussing the details and results of the core study, it will be necessary to create a common starting point by outlining the development of archival thought about selection. Therefore this first chapter is largely devoted to a comprehensive discussion of the topic. In order to clearly outline the strengths and limitations of the data reported upon in the course of the book, the second chapter details the methodology used in the study. Understanding the character of the data is critical for

1

interpreting its value in answering the question of how archivists actually select specific records for long-term retention.

To answer this essential question requires defining and assessing the importance of the many criteria archivists use in selection. Several chapters are devoted to this task because the subject is large and the level of detail is sometimes minute. As a review of archival history will show, archival theorists and practitioners have employed a large number of appraisal rationales but they have never systematically defined the criteria that these rationales are based upon, nor have they attempted to relate the criteria to one another systematically or rank criteria in order of importance. It is necessary to decide upon common definitions of criteria, and their relationship and importance to one another, if a broad consensus about how archivists select records is to exist.

Three additional points of great importance are the interrelationship of *institutional policies* to the selection of records, the *dynamics* of the decision-making process itself, and the role of *quantification* in archival selection. Policies and dynamics define the environment within which specific selection decisions are made. Because the environment's impact in molding selection decisions is decisive, the role of policy and the methodology of decision making will be examined in detail. The third point raises the question of whether quantification techniques are valid for archival selection. It is a question that has generated much interest and controversy even though quantification techniques are used in a wide variety of other information management contexts to assist in regularizing and standardizing decision making.

A better understanding of how archivists select records for long-term retention touches upon many areas of consideration and inquiry: criteria definition; interrelationship; importance; the impact of the institutional environment and decision-making formats; and the relevance of quantification techniques. Developing preliminary answers in each area is the goal of *Archival Appraisal*. The answers should serve as an important step in establishing a basis for understanding the archival selection process.

THE RATIONALE FOR DESTRUCTION

Before exploring how archivists have historically approached selection, it is worth discussing why this activity takes place. Throwing away records, irretrievably destroying information, is an activity that distresses many individuals and groups, including archivists. With some justification these individuals and groups may ask why information must be destroyed at all. Why is everything not saved?

The rationale justifying the selection of only a few records for long-term retention is based upon two premises. First, in the short run, society records more information than it actually needs. Some recorded information is ephemeral, having no more lasting importance than a telephone number jotted down on a scrap of paper. Much of the information in society is intentionally repetitive, designed to give several people immediate access to information, or to provide everyone involved in a transaction with a "record copy" of the event. The need for multiple access and numerous "record copies" of information is often short lived. Updated information makes copies of records created for convenient access obsolete. The satisfactory completion of a transaction eliminates the need for each participant in the transaction to retain documentation of the event.[1]

Although the elimination of ephemeral or intentionally redundant records may cause minor inconveniences to those who use archives, it is not likely to create serious problems for them. Much more controversial is the destruction of records containing information that is neither ephemeral nor redundant. The primary justification for this destruction is that the resources allocated by society to individuals and facilities specializing in information retention are inadequate for the indefinite preservation of all recorded information. Corporations spend only a limited sum of money on files and file clerks. Municipalities budget a fixed allocation for libraries. Colleges and universities commit only a portion of their resources to archival institutions. There is a discrete and limited amount of resources available to deal with society's information storage and retrieval tasks.

There is no theoretical reason why archivists' resources could not be increased sufficiently to preserve everything, but in the twentieth century the money available for the care of information has been inadequate to accomplish this. It does not appear that this will change. As Oliver W. Holmes noted a half century ago, "Probably society will never devote more than limited space, money, and time to the preservation of records."[2] Many archivists have complained about the baseness of a society that values its own past so little, but F. Gerald Ham, former president of the Society of American Archivists, has assessed the non-archival world's response to such archival lamentation this way: "Society must regard such broadness of spirit as profligacy, if not outright idiocy."[3]

Confronted by social realities that make choice among information a necessity, archivists have not accepted this responsibility lightly or happily. Leonard Rapport, an archivist whose familiarity with the appraisal of federal documents spans almost half a century, summed up the feelings of many archivists when he wrote, "If storage, preservation, and servicing of records cost nothing, if everything—space, material, energy, personnel—were free and in limitless supply I would advocate saving a record copy of every document, however trivial. Such a complete retention would anticipate every conceivable future use, including those we don't dream of today. But space, material, and energy, instead of being free and limitless, are becoming scarcer and costlier; and people, if not scarcer, are becoming more expensive. So, more and more, we have to think about what records we are going to be able to afford to preserve."[4] As Rapport, Ham, and Holmes all note, the necessary resources to preserve and retrieve limitless quantities of information are not now available, nor are they likely to be available in the future.[5] The archival community has accepted the difficult, but important, challenge of selecting information for long-term retention. The archival community's hope is that rational planning and decision making can eliminate, or at least minimize, the undesirable consequences of destroying information.

THE HISTORY OF ARCHIVAL APPRAISAL

Because of the profound significance of selection, archivists have worried about how decisions to retain specific information should be made. Their concern has manifested itself in an American professional literature that first began to address the question of appraisal in the 1940s, and its treatment of the topic rapidly expanded in the 1980s. Although this literature has never been completely satisfactory, it has improved over time, explaining the principles guiding appraisal and the methods used to select specific records. An appreciation of this literature is a prerequisite for understanding the archival approach towards selection.[6]

Perhaps because the shortfall between available resources and extant records was most visible in government, the National Archives of the United States served as the cradle for contemporary American appraisal thought.[7] In 1940, Philip C. Brooks presented one of the earliest published discussions on appraisal in this country. Brooks first argued for the destruction of duplicate and substantially duplicated material. Second, he attempted to define what it was that gave records "permanent value." He established three criteria in an attempt to resolve this question. The first criteria was the value that the agency or person creating the records placed on them. The second was the usefulness of the records for administrative history. The third was "historical value."[8]

Brooks' pioneering effort[9] was followed in 1944 by the work of one of his National Archives colleagues, G. Philip Bauer. Bauer staked out radical ground based on two still controversial premises. His propositions were, first, that costs should play a role in appraisal and, second, that record selection could include prioritizing information on the basis of its subsequent use.

Bauer was sharply critical of the justifications for the destruction of records commonly used in his day, and which remains frequently used today. He argued that phrases such as "ephemeral" character, "routine" records, "duplicate," and "substantially duplicated" were worn and inadequate. After analyzing and discarding each phrase, Bauer concluded, "The only candid appraisal of useless papers is a simple statement that no value is detected in them sufficient to warrant the cost of their continued preservation." Put another way, appraisal flowed from a "stern and true cost accounting."[10]

On use priorities, Bauer identified four classes of record use:

- Official reference by government agencies
- Protection of citizen's rights
- Serious research by scholars
- Satisfaction of genealogical and antiquarian curiosity.

Although Bauer acknowledged that records might be preserved for any of these categories of use, he believed the first two justified higher costs than the second two. When discussing use, Bauer established three criteria by which to judge the potential usefulness of records. He proposed that archivists look at:

- The amount and character of the information within the records
- The convenience of their arrangement
- The degree to which their textual substance is concentrated.[11]

Bauer's ideas met with varied reactions. His three criteria by which to judge usefulness were well received and quickly adopted. Bauer's prioritization of uses to which records could be put implicitly reflected his interpretation of federal priorities and, as such, hinted at the role of policy in selection. Neither he nor his contemporaries, however, developed the idea of a linkage between institutional policy and selection criteria and thus the concept remained implicit for another generation. Bauer's injection of costs into appraisal raised immediate criticism. So controversial were Bauer's ideas on cost that a rebuttal to them was included in the same publication in which they were put forth.[12]

Distinguishing Primary and Secondary Values

Important as Brooks and Bauer were to the formation of appraisal guidelines, it was their National Archives colleague, Theodore Schellenberg, who authored the touchstone of all subsequent American appraisal thought. Forming his argument a decade after Brooks and Bauer had written, Schellenberg presented a detailed appraisal taxonomy. He began by distinguishing between primary and secondary values within records. Schellenberg defined these values through use. Primary values were those uses for which the records had been originally created. Schellenberg identified three criteria to establish primary values: legal, fiscal, and administrative value.

Although Schellenberg articulated and codified primary value, he argued that records did not become truly archival until the reason for their creation had been completed. Thus secondary values, all the other possible uses to which the records might be put, were the principle concern of archival selection. In articulating secondary values, Schellenberg again divided his taxonomy into two parts.

The first, evidential values, presented documentation of the organization that created the records as well as the organization's functioning. This was evidence in the historical, not the legal, sense. The three criteria used to establish evidential value were the position of each office in the organization's hierarchy, the function of each office in the organization, and the activities carried out to perform the function. For practical purposes the records identified as important by Schellenberg's evidential criteria are the records necessary to write an administrative history of an organization.

Schellenberg labelled the other component of secondary values informational values. Informational values encompassed information found in a broad range of records that documented specific persons, things, and phenomena considered "important." Importance was determined by ascertaining the information's uniqueness, concentration (form), and number of different users served by it. Schellenberg's typology reflected and elaborated upon some of Brooks' and Bauer's earlier ideas but excluded Bauer's emphasis on costs and prioritization of uses. Schellenberg's taxonomy was complex, but even in the 1950s archivists realized that appraisal was a difficult task that involved a number of criteria.[13]

Schellenberg's taxonomy served a generation of American archivists as their primary explanation of appraisal. Although his writing, as well as that of Bauer and Brooks, reflected the unique problems of the federal government, the logic and clarity of Schellenberg's ideas led archivists in a variety of bureaucratic settings to apply his appraisal standards to nongovernmental records.[14] So influential was Schellenberg's work that for almost 20 years research on the topic virtually stopped.

Broadening Archival Criteria

When, in the 1970s, archivists again turned their attention to appraisal, those writing on the subject usually had not worked at the

National Archives nor did they have their primary experience working with federal records. The first effort to revive writing on selection began when the Society of American Archivists (SAA) determined that there was a need for manuals relating to several basic archival functions, including appraisal.[15] The responsibility for writing a basic manual on appraisal fell to Maynard J. Brichford. A college and university archivist, Brichford approached his task with a perspective that went beyond the concerns of a particular institution or environment. He looked at appraisal in the broadest sense and incorporated into his work a range of criteria that he believed was useful in selection.

In place of Schellenberg's model, Brichford presented a complex array of appraisal ideas based upon four fundamental concerns:

- The characteristics of the records
- Administrative values
- Research values
- Archival values.

Each of these concerns was further subdivided. Listed under the first, record characteristics, were age, volume, form, functional characteristics, evidential characteristics, and informational characteristics. The second concern, administrative values, restated Schellenberg's primary values, those being administrative, fiscal, and legal concerns. Brichford's third concern, research values, was conceptualized as having seven criteria: uniqueness, credibility, understandability, time span, accessibility, frequency of use, and type and quality of use. Finally, under archival values, Brichford included the record's relationship to other records, and reintroduced the stern accounting of Bauer by including processing, preservation, and storage costs.[16] Brichford's manual was an intellectual tour that surveyed the appraisal landscape. Although much of the scenery was as Brooks, Bauer, and Schellenberg had described it, Brichford made clear that their view from the National Archives was not identical to the view of all archivists.

The Role of Institutional Policy

Although Brichford's volume addressed the long-standing archival concern regarding the selection of specific records for retention, attention again began to be focused on the role of the preserving institution. A few years earlier F. Gerald Ham had resurrected and broadened Bauer's implicit recognition regarding the role of institutional policy in selection. Ham began his 1974 presidential address before the Society of American Archivists with the words, "Our most important and intellectually demanding task as archivists is to make an informed selection of information that will provide the future with a representative record of human experience in our time. But why must we do it so badly?"[17] Ham's professional critique included not just the appraisal of specific records, but the entire process through which archivists document society.

Ham restated, refined, and to some extent redirected his 1974 critique though a 1980 plenary address to SAA, and in a core session paper he delivered at the Society of American Archivists 1982 meeting.[18] Ham's presentations set the stage for continued work on the traditional appraisal concern about how to select specific records. He also energized archivists to begin exploring the overall dimensions of the information universe and the effects of institutional policies on appraisal.

Ham personally was most interested in exploring the documentation of large social questions through institutional and interinstitutional policies. As part of the goal of collection management, Ham proposed a framework of interinstitutional cooperation in which archival institutions would create documentation networks. These networks would be based upon complementary institutional core-collection policies and cooperatively developed, interrelated and noncompetitive subject specializations that would be broadly defined but housed in particular institutions. Such a network, he hoped, would lead to the establishment of rational regional and even national collecting goals. Achieving this goal of specific core-collection goals and broadly based subject responsibilities required two important precursor steps: institutions first needed to understand what it is that they actually documented and, secondly, to rationalize their own acquisition and appraisal procedures.[19]

Assessing the Collection Analysis Process

An approach toward the information gathering and analysis activities Ham advocated was explained by two authors, Gloria Thompson and Judith Endelman. Thompson described a project conducted at the Minnesota Historical Society in which all existing collections were examined and categorized by topical emphasis. Topics were selected from a list of 18 subject categories drawn up by the Society itself. The collective profile was used to display strengths and dispel myths about what the collections documented, and to rationalize the Society's collecting policies. Endelman described the collection analysis process and its policy implications in more depth. She drew upon not only the Minnesota experience, but also upon collection analysis projects conducted at the State Historical Society of Wisconsin and the University of Michigan's Bentley Historical Library.[20]

Another attempt to explain the planning Ham called for was written by Jutta Reed-Scott, who approached the problem by applying the collection management literature of librarians to archives. In a companion piece, Faye Phillips applied Reed-Scott's approach to the development of collecting policies. Phillips outlined a nine-point collecting plan that included:

- A broad statement of purpose
- Recognition of the types of programs supported through collecting
- Clientele
- Collection priorities and limitations
- Cooperative agreements
- Statements regarding resource sharing
- A deaccessioning policy
- Procedures to monitor the development of the collection
- Review guidelines.[21]

Ham's broad challenge to look at the process by which society is documented not only led archivists to think about the impact of institutional policy on archival selection, but also to consider the total information universe from which archivists draw documentation. Ham addressed this point by raising two issues. Archivists had long been advised to evaluate individual records in terms of overall record keeping systems. Ham transcended this advice by asking archivists to look at the content of all related information, whatever the character of the recording media, when selecting documents for long-term retention. He also recommended that archival selection include consideration of the value of one record source to serve as a substitute for another.[22]

Joan K. Haas, Helen Willa Samuels and Barbara Trippel Simmons jointly built upon Ham's observations regarding the information universe and sought to expand them to include the processes by which information is created. In a work designed to aid in the archival selection of records regarding science and technology, Haas, Samuels, and Simmons stated the premise that, "To appraise effectively archivists need to understand that the nature of the scientific and technological process and the complex patterns of communication and funding affect the existence and location of records."[23] The authors' observation challenged archivists to examine the functional characteristics and communication patterns of the records creators and went far beyond the more common advice that archivists study institutional history.

The most ambitious specific strategy that emerged to implement Ham's call for a reconsideration of the broad context of archival selection was an idea labelled *documentation strategy*. Helen Samuels, as well as Larry Hackman and Joan Warnow-Blewett, have introduced the idea that the interrelatedness of modern institutional documentation requires the development of rational interinstitutional plans to adequately document an issue, activity, or geographic area. As Helen Samuels rhetorically asked, "How many archival repositories does it take to document the complexities of the moonshot?"[24] Samuels laid out the theoretical underpinnings of documentation strategies, Joan Warnow-Blewett wrote a documentation strategy case study, and Larry Hackman described the process through which a documentation strategy is established.[25] Although the overall applicability of documentation strategy is still being debated, it represents a development in the effort to both consider the nature of records and to establish interinstitutional collecting policies.[26]

Drawing on European Tradition

The concern American archivists developed in the 1970s and 1980s for the impact of institutional policies and the nature of the record universe appears to have a much longer tradition in Europe. Although references to European sources in the English literature are few, the German Hans Booms has published a lengthy article that reviews 80 years of German thinking on these matters, and includes a controversial personal argument. Premising his analysis on the belief that there is no such thing as absolute value in information, Booms argued that the value of all information is relative and is determined by comparing the information to "value coordinates." Having established this premise, he traced the development of these coordinates in Germany.[27]

In the nineteenth century, archivists' value coordinates were legalistic. In the twentieth century, because of the influence of historians, the value coordinates guiding archivists became historical. After almost 60 years of trying to develop satisfactory value coordinates based upon the importance of government records and the values of history, some German archivists abandoned all efforts to link historical research to archival selection. Booms himself proposed that the solution to the problem of what to save is for the archivist to document the entire spectrum of social phenomena. Booms recommended that the level of documentation for a particular phenomenon should be based upon the importance the society creating the records gave to that phenomenon. Although he conceded that letting the past decide upon its own documentary heritage is not a perfect solution, Booms argued that just as public opinion is the ultimate legitimization of political authority, so too public opinion can be the ultimate arbiter for selection.

Booms demonstrated that the problems regarding the impact of institutional policy and the nature of the documentary universe that American archivists have wrestled with since the 1970s are also of concern to European archivists. While many American and European archivists have wrestled with these difficult problems, a second group of archivists continued to focus primarily upon the older problem of how to actually choose records for retention. F. Gerald Ham was less influential in this second research area. At one point he dismissed the need for extensive new research into actual record selection, saying, "Traditional appraisal canons will continue to serve archivists well in arriving at a compelling justification [for retaining records]."[28] Ham, however, may not have been as complacent about the unimportance of research regarding specific record selection as this sweeping quote would imply. In the same speech he also mentioned that "archivists must learn to attach a price tag to appraisal decisions," and thus argued for including the costs of processing and preservation when selecting specific records for archival storage.[29]

Specific Record Selection: Paper

Others, however, have been more forceful than Ham in asserting their belief that the archival community needs to examine the criteria through which it selects specific records as "archival." Frank Boles and Julia Young presented an examination of appraisal criteria for traditional paper records. They attempted to develop a taxonomy that synthesized the time-honored ideas of Schellenberg, the more radical ideas of Bauer, the wealth of criteria proposed by Brichford, and their own notions of what elements composed record selection. Boles and Young conceived of appraisal as consisting of three *modules*:

- Value of information
- Costs of retention
- Implications of the appraisal recommendation.

Under each broad heading they presented a complex taxonomy of components, subcomponents, and elements. Although their work recognized and pointed to the importance of institutional policy and the universe of documentation, it focused upon actual record selection, rather than the policy elements that informed such selection.[30]

Michael Cook, a British author, has also offered contemporary guidance on picking specific records for archives. Cook focused on the importance of Schellenberg's informational values, while at the same time dismissing Schellenberg's concept of evidential value. Cook challenged the usefulness of evidential value, finding something "suspicious" about it and wryly noting:

> [Archival descriptions] depend on the archivist's ability to establish and write down the administrative history of the organisation he is working on. The training of an archivist, in most countries, also depends considerably on learning national administrative, institutional or legal history. From this we can see that evidential values correspond very closely to one of the archivist's main professional preoccupations. Is it possible to conclude that an archivist's tendency to preserve, first of all and perhaps mainly, the materials for the institutional history of an organization, is based upon a delusion, and that they

should be concentrating instead on identifying and preserving records which give useful information on relevant subjects?

Cook concludes his criticism of Schellenberg with a final observation that, "Such a view might be reinforced by the fact that, unlike the 'evidential' concept, [informational value] is easy to understand and remember."[31]

Having criticized evidential value, Cook made a few observations about the selection of records, reestablishing themes stated earlier by the Americans Maynard Brichford and G. Philip Bauer. Cook divided all selection decisions into two categories: records to be kept forever, and records to be kept for as long as they last. In the former category he placed national treasures, documents "'worth a visit' [in the words of the guidebooks] by the public."[32] In the latter category were placed most everything else in an archives. The distinction between the two categories is, for Cook, a mixture of finances and use statistics. He asked what it will cost, how many people will find it useful, and advocated the inclusion of a cost-use ratio in appraisal decisions. Although Cook conceded that this is not the whole appraisal equation, he argued that it is a necessary component in any decision.[33]

Appraising Machine-Readable Records

While Boles and Young, as well as Cook, discussed paper records, Harold Naugler wrote a detailed manual discussing the appraisal of machine-readable records. Naugler divided appraisal into two broad categories, content analysis and technical analysis. An archivist, Naugler advised, should first analyze content using the traditional elements of uniqueness of information or format, level of aggregation, and importance of the information. To these traditional criteria, Naugler added electronic-oriented criteria such as manipulation of information and linkage potential.[34] Naugler's technical criteria went beyond previously expressed concerns regarding the continuing readability of the data on available hardware and software, and the adequacy of supporting documentation to explain the data. He advocated considering the costs of acquiring, processing, preserving, and servicing (reference use of) information. He also considered the impact of use restrictions, both in terms of lessening the information's value because it could not be used for many years, and in relation to the cost of producing a public copy of information that excludes closed information such as names or other personal identifiers. Although these technical criteria were designed explicitly for machine-readable records, the criteria also appeared applicable in some circumstances to records in other formats.[35]

"Inherent Values" Controversy

In a recent publication David Bearman has called into question the whole approach of the archival community in selecting records. Bearman rejects the validity of "the concept of values inherent in records" as a selection tool. He finds it methodologically inadequate for coping with the mass of records available for selection and believes it leads to "a false impression of being based in cost-benefit analysis." As a replacement for the ideas and techniques he rejects, Bearman suggests the use of risk management techniques in the archival selection of records, coupled with a wide-ranging debate over the purposes for which information is stored and the ultimate goals of archives.[36]

Although Bearman's concept is interesting, risk management techniques may be as difficult to use in practice as cost-benefit analysis. Risk management assumes that a rational decision can be made regarding the potential harm that might occur should particular information be lost. In some settings where archival missions are relatively narrow this may be a fairly straightforward decision. A corporate archives, for example, might be able to calculate the potential legal liabilities should certain information be available and come to a rational decision regarding the risk involved in destroying it. An archives with a broad agenda, however, particularly one dedicated to preserving information of cultural importance, would have a difficult time reaching such a decision. How would an archivist calculate the risk of cultural loss to society should a particular piece of information be destroyed? From where would the archivist derive the value coordinates needed to make such a decision?

CONCLUSION

The history of archival selection is a long and complex one. Thoughtful archivists on several continents have wrestled with the question of how to choose the small portion of the overall quantity of created information that will be held for long-term use. The methods through which archivists select specific records and the manner in which the broader environment informs the selection of specific records have been defined in ever increasing detail, with the decade of the 1980s proving to be a particularly fertile period among American archivists interested in exploring this area.

What has been lacking from this discussion, however, has been empirical examinations of how archivists actually carry out their specific selection responsibilities. Although thoughtful archivists have reflected individually upon their activity in this area, and informal communication has added breadth to many authors' perspectives, there has been no empirical research regarding selection. Archival theory about selection consists largely of the thoughtful, but personal, reflections of several archivists. The commonality between these authors' experiences and the experiences of the vast majority of archivists who have not written on selection is uncertain. Uncertain also are ways to resolve conflicts that have emerged in a literature based largely on individual experience.

Archival theory about selection has not been informed by a systematic examination of practice. The data presented in this book was collected through a pioneering empirical study designed to advance theory through a better knowledge of selection practice coupled with extended discussion with practitioners. The data were collected and are presented in the hope that practice may help resolve and clarify a number of issues that abstract theory cannot adequately address.

Endnotes

1. Legal requirements often complicate the ability to dispose of documents after the completion of a transaction, but the principle remains clear despite legal complications.
2. Oliver W. Holmes, "The Evaluation and Preservation of Business Records," *American Archivist* 1 (October 1938): 171.
3. F. Gerald Ham, "Archival Choices: Managing the Historical Record in an Age of Abundance," *American Archivist* 47 (Winter 1984): 12.
4. Leonard Rapport, "No Grandfather Clause: Reappraising Accessioned Records," *American Archivist* 44 (Spring 1981): 143.
5. Some archivists have argued that various technological advances will allow significantly improved retention of records at a reasonable cost. See, for example, William Nolte, "High-Speed Text Search Systems and Their Archival Implications," *American Archivist* 50 (Fall 1987): 580-584. Although the possibility exists that a technological "fix" may solve some current problems, often the usefulness of new technologies in solving old problems is limited by the new problems the technological "fix" creates. In the case of computerized records, the short life of the magnetic signal upon the media and, more importantly, the dynamic changes in commonly used hardware and software makes ten- to twenty-year-old data unreadable.
6. Expressions of dissatisfaction with the appraisal literature are summed up in Richard Berner's statement that he omitted appraisal from the history of archives he authored because of "the primitive nature of its development." Richard C. Berner, *Archival Theory and Practice in the United States: A Historical Analysis* (Seattle: University of Washington Press, 1983): 6.
7. An alternative explanation, that the sheer bulk of the federal government's records required that something be done, does not appear as likely. In the 1940s archivists who collected business records also realized that their collecting efforts had discovered a huge quantity of paper, but the optimistic assumption that the business community could

be convinced to contribute the necessary resources to preserve the records may have led these archivists away from serious consideration of appraisal criteria. Francis X. Blouin, Jr., "An Agenda for the Appraisal of Business Records," in Nancy E. Peace, ed., *Archival Choices: Managing the Historical Record in an Age of Abundance* (Lexington, MA: Lexington Books, 1984): 64-65.

8. Philip C. Brooks, "The Selection of Records for Preservation," *American Archivist* 3 (October 1940): 228-234. Brooks' seemingly bland remarks regarding the destruction of near-duplicate and duplicate material were, in fact, controversial in that they contradicted the advice of the British archivist Hilary Jenkinson. Of near duplicates, Jenkinson had stated, "The idea that any document can be considered to come near duplicating another, unless it is almost word for word the same, is simply erroneous." As for word-for-word duplicates, Jenkinson concluded, "...it is impossible to lay down any procedure for determining whether one document is the duplicate of another except a page for page and a line for line collation; and it is very doubtful whether such work will not prove so expensive as to make destruction hardly worthwhile." Hilary Jenkinson, *A Manual of Archive Administration* (London: Percy Lund, Humphries & Co., 1937): 144; 143.

9. Emmett J. Leahy had written an earlier article which detailed the administrative processes within government for record destruction, but that article explicitly excluded consideration of the criteria through which permanent value could be determined. Emmett J. Leahy, "Reduction of Public Records," *American Archivist* 3 (January 1940): 13. Margaret Cross Norton also wrote presciently regarding appraisal in the 1940s but, perhaps because her thoughts were published in the relatively obscure *Illinois Libraries*, they did not have the professional impact of the writing coming from the National Archives. Margaret Cross Norton, "The Disposal of Records," *Illinois Libraries* 26 (March 1944): 120-124, reprinted in Thornton W. Mitchell, ed., *Norton on Archives: The Writings of Margaret Cross Norton on Archival & Records Management* (Carbondale: Southern Illinois University Press, 1975): 231-246.

10. G. Philip Bauer, *The Appraisal of Current and Recent Records: Staff Information Paper #13* (Washington: National Archives, 1946): 3-5.

11. Ibid., 6-7.

12. Ibid., 22-25.

13. Schellenberg first laid out his ideas in Theodore R. Schellenberg, *The Appraisal of Modern Public Records National Archives Bulletin #8* (Washington: National Archives, 1956), partially reprinted in Maygene F. Daniels and Timothy Walch, eds., *A Modern Archives Reader: Basic Readings on Archival Theory and Practice* (Washington: National Archives & Records Administration, 1984): 57-70.

14. For a more detailed discussion of the governmental context of Schellenberg's thought and the limitations that are inherent in it, see Frank Boles and Julia Young, "Exploring the Black Box: The Appraisal of University Administrative Records," *American Archivist* 48 (1985): 122-124. Beverly Hart, Stephen Ellis, and Ian Pritchard also note the effect of U.S. government legislation on Schellenberg's guidelines in "The Appraisal and Scheduling of Government Records: A New

Approach by the Australian Archives," *American Archivist* 50 (1987): 597 fn 10.

15.   C.F.W. Coker, Jan Shelton Danis, and Robert M. Warner, forward to Maynard J. Brichford, *Archives & Manuscripts: Appraisal & Accessioning* (Chicago: Society of American Archivists, 1977): v.

16.   Ibid., 2-11.

17.   F. Gerald Ham, "The Archival Edge," *American Archivist* 38 (January 1975): 5.

18.   F. Gerald Ham, "Archival Strategies for the Post-Custodial Era," *American Archivist* 44 (Summer 1981): 207-216, and "Archival Choices: Managing the Historical Record in the Age of Abundance," *American Archivist* 47 (Winter 1984): 11-22.

19.   Ham, "Archival Choices", 13-15.

20.   Gloria A. Thompson, "From Profile to Policy: A Minnesota Historical Society Case Study in Collection Development," *Midwestern Archivist* 8 (1983 no. 2): 29-39, and Judith E. Endelman, "Looking Backward to Plan for the Future: Collection Analysis for Manuscript Repositories," *American Archivist* 50 (Summer 1987): 340-355. For a discussion of another project similar to those discussed by Thompson and Endelman, see David Levine, "The Appraisal Policy of the Ohio State Archives," *American Archivist* 47 (Summer 1984): 291-293.

21.   Jutta Reed-Scott, "Collection Management Strategies for Archivists," *American Archivist* 47 (1984): 23-29, and Faye Phillips, "Developing Collecting Policies for Manuscript Collections," *American Archivist* 47 (1984): 39-42.

22.   Ham, "Archival Choices," 15-16. Ham was particularly concerned about archivists' tendency to ignore information found in printed and other secondary sources when they evaluated the need to retain information found in primary sources.

23.   Joan K. Haas, Helen Willa Samuels, and Barbara Trippel Simmons, *Appraising the Records of Modern Science and Technology: A Guide* (Cambridge: Massachusetts Institute of Technology, 1985): 23.

24.   Helen Willa Samuels, "Who Controls the Past," *American Archivist* 49 (1986): 112.

25.   Larry Hackman and Joan Warnow-Blewett, "The Documentation Strategy Process: A Model and a Case Study," *American Archivist* 50 (1987): 12-47. For another view of how a documentation strategy could be implemented see Philip N. Alexander and Helen W. Samuels, "The Roots of 128: A Hypothetical Documentation Strategy," *American Archivist* 50 (1987): 518-531.

26.   Discussion of the applicability of interinstitutional documentation strategies in the context of institutional goals and priorities is contained in both Judith E. Endelman, "Looking Backward to Plan for the Future," and Frank Boles, "Mix Two Parts Interest to One Part Information and Appraise Until Done: Understanding Contemporary Record Selection Processes," *American Archivist* 50 (1987): 356-368. See especially 363-367.

27.   Hans Booms, "Society and the Formation of a Documentary Heritage: Issues in the Appraisal of Documentary Sources," reprinted in English translation in *Archivaria* 24 (1987): 69-107. Booms article was originally

presented as an address to the German Archives Conference in 1971
and was published in Germany a year later. In the early 1980s a few
American publications, notably Nancy E. Peace, "Deciding What to
Save: Fifty Years of Theory and Practice," in Peace, ed., *Archival
Choices,* see particularly 9-13, brought Booms' article to the attention of
English-speaking archivists. Peace, however, worked from an English
translation of only the summary of Booms' article (Ibid., xi). The full
text of Booms' work did not appear in English until its publication in
Archivaria.

28. Ham, "Archival Choices," 15.
29. Ibid., 15-16. Quotation on page 16.
30. Boles and Young, "Exploring the Black Box," 121-140.
31. Michael Cook, *The Management of Information from Archives*
     (Shaftesbury: Gower, 1986): 71. Susan D. Steinwall, "Appraisal and the
     FBI Files Case: For Whom Do Archivists Retain Records?" *American.
     Archivist* 49 (1986): 52-63, makes a very similar point on the tendency of
     archivists to overvalue evidential criteria.
32. Ibid., 72.
33. Ibid., 73. Reference has already been made to Bauer's pathbreaking work.
     Maynard Brichford expressed a sentiment very similar to Cook's in a
     1979 address to SAA entitled, "Seven Sinful Thoughts." Among
     Brichford's impious suggestions was the dictum, "let them rot," adding
     "The millions of cubic feet of records in archival custody cannot be pre-
     served forever." Maynard Brichford, "Seven Sinful Thoughts," *American
     Archivist* 43 (1980): 14.
34. Harold Naugler, *The Archival Appraisal of Machine-Readable Records: A
     RAMP Study with Guidelines* (Paris: General Information Programme
     and UNISIST, United Nations Education, Scientific and Cultural Orga-
     nization, 1984): 39-55.
35. Ibid., 57-61. See also David Bearman, *Electronic Record Guidelines: A
     Manual for Policy Development and Implementation* (np; Archives and
     Museum Informatics, nd. ca. 1990): 56-65. Bearman, 116-124, includes
     an extensive bibliography of the literature regarding machine-readable
     records.
36. David Bearman, "Archival Methods," *Archives and Museum Informatics
     Technical Reports*, 3 (1989): 6-16; quotations from p. 16.

2

Project Methodology

The archival community has devoted considerable thought to the selection of records. Despite this, before the project from which *Archival Appraisal* grew, no systematic study had ever been undertaken to compare the attitudes and beliefs of archivists at different institutions. To develop initial answers to some of the research issues in selection, the project examined four issues. First, by polling a large number of archivists, it attempted to determine if common selection elements were in use in different archival settings. Second, the project sought to develop a taxonomy to interrelate those common selection elements discovered. Third, the project looked at selection practice in a number of archival institutions to determine how archival selection decisions were made. Fourth, the project explored the possible use of quantification in selection, both as a device to help clarify policy regarding selection and as a practical selection tool.

This chapter discusses how these issues were investigated by presenting the project's research design. Specifically, the chapter discusses three major components of the project: the construction of a manual to guide participants, the selection of test sites, and the orientation and research activities undertaken after the project was underway. The results obtained through the research design will be discussed in the subsequent chapters.

TEST MANUAL

Although its creation preceded the formal beginning of the project, the writing of the project manual was critical to the project and its results.[1] The 41-page manual outlined for participants what they were to do and how they were to record their activity and thoughts. The specific instructions, and the underlying assumptions found in the manual, shaped the project.

Establishing a systematic method to solicit and compare various archivists' ideas about selection posed significant challenges. Archivists shared no commonly accepted list of terms that defined the elements upon which archival selection was based. Archivists, furthermore, had never agreed upon a common taxonomy that classified the activities or concepts involved in selection. The goal was to create a manual that established a common terminology, a common intellectual framework, and a common evaluative procedure. To obtain an orderly response to the questions the project posed about selection, a preliminary set of defined selection elements had to be developed. Identifying these elements and determining participants' reactions to this preliminary work in day-to-day archival practice created several problems that had to be addressed before research could be undertaken.

Participants were asked to evaluate this work subjectively and also to apply it to real record selection tasks, recording the results and comparing them to results obtained from their customary selection procedures. Participants agreed to use the manual as an arbitrary authority for actual selection, temporarily suspending their experience-based comments and criticisms. Although it was designed as a research tool to focus a discussion of selection among archivists, significant work went into its design so that it might also be, insofar as possible, a workable selection method that reflected the existing archival literature, rather than simply an arbitrary set of definitions and procedures.

Developing Preliminary Terms

Resolving the basic problem of identifying and defining common descriptive terms and establishing a taxonomy through which to describe the various component judgments that archivists make was accomplished by relying upon the previously published work of Boles and Young.[2] The task, however, called for additional development of this work. Some of the problems involved in developing the preliminary terms can be understood by looking at the problem of defining the word *appraisal*.

As it is used by most archivists, *appraisal* has come to mean evaluating the informational content of a record with an eye toward determining whether or not it is sufficiently important to merit long-term retention.[3] When the term *appraisal* was used in the manual to include noninformational forms of analysis such as costs, several archivists participating in the project objected because to them that was not *appraisal*, despite the discussion of such ideas in the literature. To avoid this particular semantic difficulty, the term *selection* is used to describe a process that includes not only the appraisal of information, but consideration of costs, institutional policies and goals, and other factors that affect an archivist's decision regarding whether or not records will be retained.[4] The difficulty of obtaining consensus among participants regarding the definition of appraisal foreshadowed a series of other definitional problems that had to be resolved in order to be sure that all participants in the project meant the same thing when they used a particular word or phrase.

Although the terms, their definition, and the taxonomy employed in the instructions will all be subject to review later, it is useful to present here an overview of what was used. The taxonomy's basic structure consisted of three conceptual groups, called modules, originally labelled *Value-of-Information*, *Costs-of-Retention*, and *Policy Implications*, and hereafter shortened for convenience.

FIGURE 2-1.   Value-of-Information Module

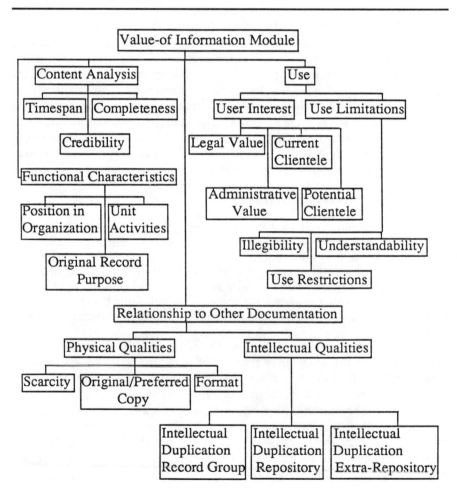

The *Information* module brought together the ideas used by archivists to evaluate the nature, quality, independence, and usefulness of the information contained in a specific set of records. It was organized around four conceptually related clusters of 19 elements:

- Functional characteristics
- Content analysis
- Relationship to other documentation
- Use.

The 19 elements were identified and defined primarily from the archival literature. Functional characteristic and content analysis elements were drawn largely from Schellenberg's writings on evidential and informational value, as amplified by Maynard Brichford. Relationship to other documentation came out of the writings of Brooks, Ham, Samuels, and Blouin. Use relied partly on Schellenberg's idea of primary values, Bauer, Naugler, and Boles and Young's published ideas on the subject.

FIGURE 2-2.   Costs-of-Retention Module

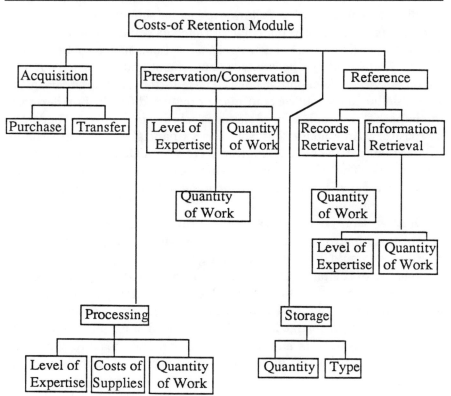

Identifying and Measuring Costs

The *Costs* module consisted of 13 elements which articulated and linked the many expenses archival institutions incur if records are accepted. The elements incorporated the belief that the expense of preserving information should be a part of the selection decision. Costs were organized around five conceptual clusters:

- Acquisition
- Processing
- Preservation/conservation
- Storage
- Reference.

The first four clusters are rooted primarily in the writings of G. Philip Bauer and Maynard Brichford, while the fifth, *reference*, is drawn from the work of Harold Naugler and Boles and Young.

Measuring costs is not as straightforward as it would seem. The appealingly simple approach of looking at dollars and cents ignores several problems. The overall resources available to different archives are diverse, encompassing factors such as personnel, time, and space. Accounting encompasses many factors such as volunteer labor, student assistants, and nonline budgetary considerations such as maintenance or utility bills paid by a centralized department and not costed out on a fee-for-service or some other basis. These factors make rendering the actual dollar and cents costs in many archives difficult. Furthermore, the impact of a specific sum of money is relative to the overall budget of a repository. An amount that would be a financial windfall in Urbana, Illinois may create only a slight stir in New York City's more expensive atmosphere. The effect of a particular expense varies greatly from institution to institution. (We are indebted to William Maher for sharpening our thinking on this point.)

Rather than using dollars, the project compared the average expenses an institution incurred and the projected expenses that specific records would involve. Comparing generalized expectations regarding costs with the particular circumstances created by specific records represented was a way to acknowledge relative differences in budget, institutional size, and other economically related factors without requiring participants to engage in extensive financial analysis. Although the resulting analysis was admittedly a less precise measure than true financial analysis, it was an adequate measure for the purposes of this study.[5]

Assessing the Implications

Implications incorporated into the selection decision 13 additional concerns regarding both the impact of a particular recommendation upon the institution's general selection practices and the interaction between a particular selection decision and the overall goals of the archives or its parent institution. Implications was divided into two broad clusters: external and internal. Intellectually, it was not rooted in the archival literature, but rather in ideas taken from the decision-making literature found in various sociological sources.

FIGURE 2-3:   Policy Implications Module

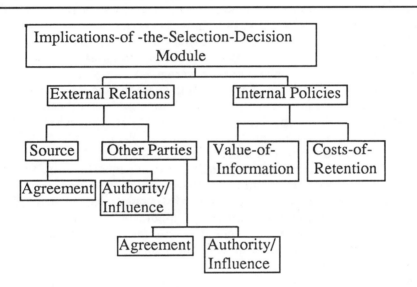

Taken together the three modules represent a taxonomy that attempted to classify the elements used by archivists to select records. In the abstract the system was cumbersome and awkward. Nevertheless it reflected the broad but poorly organized insights archivists brought to selection. Over a half century, archivists had presented a number of concerns that they believed affected a particular selection decision. A taxonomy rooted in that heritage was of necessity weighted down by including so many factors. As a practical selection tool, the taxonomy was even more limited. The intellectual awkwardness of the system was compounded by the practical unwieldiness of consciously considering so many elements. Despite the framework's limitations as a practical tool, it created an intellectual vehicle that allowed the project to address questions regarding the validity and relative importance of various selection elements in theory and in practice.

Quantitative Measurement Conundrums

Having created a preliminary selection system, the research design required a measuring device to gauge participants' opinions regarding this system and its application. To accomplish this the design linked the preliminary selection system to a quantitative measurement methodology. Using numbers had two inherent disadvantages. First, it meant introducing participants to an unfamiliar numerical scheme. This was a task of considerable magnitude, which at least one participant considered to take more time and energy than the substantive discussion of selection itself. The second disadvantage was the false appearance of certainty numbers gave to the results. The nonrandom character of the site selection process and the small size of the sample relative to the overall population meant that the numerical results obtained would not be statistically significant. No matter how often this was stated, it was apparent that some individuals would attach statistical significance to the results simply because numbers were used.

In spite of these drawbacks, using numbers made it possible to discuss several issues more precisely than would have been possible using prose descriptions. Numbers were used not to establish statistically valid observations, but to penetrate and clarify the linguistic veil that surrounded most prior discussions of selection.

The manual incorporated quantification at several points. Test site participants were first asked to rank each element in the taxonomy in order of importance on a scale ranging from one to four. A score of one represented an element of little or no importance in selections in the participating institution. An element scored four represented a critical part of the selection process, some factor upon which selection decisions frequently hinged.

From Quantity to Quality

This ranking exercise was valuable for two reasons. Qualitative, although tentative, conclusions could be drawn regarding the relative importance of selection elements from the cumulative average values assigned to each score. In addition, the numbers themselves could be used as part of a more complex mathematical methodology. Specifically, these rank scores were used as multipliers to increase the value of the numerical score that participating archivists assigned for each element as they evaluated particular records. These element scores, multiplied by the element weight, were combined in an algebraic equation designed to calculate the final major mathematical idea incorporated into the manual: a final selection score. As originally conceived, the equation tested the applicability of a classic cost-benefit ratio in appraisal decisions. (See the beginning of chapter 4 for a more detailed explanation.)

Reporting results was a far more straightforward process than confronting the problems of numerical analysis, taxonomy, and elements. The manual included standard forms on which the information regarding the application of the system to specific selection decisions could be recorded. The reporting form followed the basic structure of the taxonomy and the quantitative methodology, asking participants to "fill in the blanks." In addition, a standard form for accumulating information regarding participating institutions was distributed.

The test manual, in its entirety, was a complex document that incorporated a broad number of assumptions and techniques. Identifying and defining elements, creating a taxonomy, incorporating a numerical scheme, and establishing reporting structures represented a task that included accumulated wisdom, assumptions, assertions, and, occasionally, blind guesses. The manual, however, controlled and shaped what was to come.

TEST SITES

Important as the manual was, equally important were the institutions asked to use it. The character of the test participants was critical in shaping the project's results. In selecting test sites, nonscientific, nonrandom criteria were employed. The first objective was to identify specific archives that represented various types of archival institutions. Five types of archival institutions were identified:

- College and university
- Governmental
- Religious
- Business
- Manuscript.

The second objective was to locate specific institutions in each category that had experienced selection staff who would apply their hard-won insights to the questions and implications of the manual. A third objective was to select test sites that would be demographically diverse in easily quantifiable areas such as staff size, program age, quantity of repository holdings, and overall budget.

Although the three major objectives of institution type, staff experience, and demographic diversity were the predominant factors in site selection, budgetary realities also played a role in inviting institutions to participate. First, the test sites had to devote significant staff time to the project without reimbursement. Second, a decision that the project's coordinators should visit participating archivists at or near the participants' institution prior to the beginning of the test, and after the test's conclusion, led to a concern about the size of the travel budget. This concern argued for establishing test sites in either the upper Midwest or deep South, near the two project coordinators, or for establishing test sites in cities that are major air transportation hubs. Although travel considerations were never allowed to become determining factors, they did serve to establish certain underlying preferences.

Eventually, 14 test sites were established. The sites met three basic criteria of institutional type, experience, and demographic diversity. Included were three college or university archives: Bowling Green State University, Massachusetts Institute of Technology, and New York University; two business archives: Chase Manhattan Bank, and Kraft, Inc.; three religious organizations: the Billy Graham Archives, Episcopal Church of Canada, and the Salvation Army Archives; three manuscript repositories: the University of Minnesota's Immigration History and Research Center, the Mississippi State Archives Manuscript Division, and the New York Public Library; and three public archives: the New York State Archives, the Alabama State Archives, and the Illinois State Archives.[6]

This group of test sites differed in accordance with the other selection criteria. Their professional staffs averaged about nine people, but ranged from three to 30. The typical test-site archive had existed for about 37 years, the oldest founded in 1901, the newest established in 1984. On average, the institutions held about 14,000 linear feet of material, but the smallest held a mere 650 linear feet, while the largest held 64,000 linear feet. On average, the test sites accessioned about 700 linear feet of new material in their last year for which a report was available; however, the range was considerable, from a low of 163 linear feet to a high of 3,738 linear feet. Although the test sites averaged approximately 7,500 research visits a year, the range was again large, from a low of 663 to a high of 59,924. By any measure the institutions selected were diverse, although when compared with national statistics they were larger and busier than the typical archive.[7]

Test Procedures

To discover any overwhelming problems, the New York State Archives and the Chase Manhattan Bank archives pretested the manual for three weeks during the summer of 1987. The results of the pretest served as the basis for modifications made to the manual mailed to all test participants in September 1987. Participants used the test methodology for eight weeks. As in the pretest, they employed it in tandem with normal selection procedures on whatever material came through the archives in the normal course of affairs.[8] As in the pretest, participants attended an orientation session led by one or both of the project coordinators before they actually began to use the manual. At the end of the test period a principal investigator visited with participants to discuss their results.

CONCLUSION

The methodology devised, although it did not offer the prospect of answering all of the pressing questions in selection, did address a large number of these important questions. Although subsequent work eventually pointed out conceptual flaws and shortcomings that should be corrected in any subsequent interinstitutional study of selection, as a pilot methodology in an area where no previous work had been done, the project's overall approach worked as well as or better than could be expected. By and large participants could make sense of it and, although not necessarily without complaint, could report back results that were comparable. Based on those results the methodology can be considered successful.

Endnotes

1. The author wishes to acknowledge the assistance of the Bentley Historical Library of the University of Michigan in supplying funding that enabled the preparation of the basic text of the manual as well as the undertaking of the significant pregrant activities that led to NHPRC funding.
2. Frank Boles and Julia Marks Young, "Exploring the Black Box: The Appraisal of University Administrative Records," *American Archivist*, 48 (1985): 121-140.
3. Appraisal is defined as, "The process of determining the value and thus the disposition of records based upon their current administrative, legal, and fiscal use; their evidential and informational or research value; their arrangement; and their relationship to other records" in Frank B. Evans, et. al. "A Basic Glossary for Archivists, Manuscripts Curators, and Records Managers," *American Archivist* 37 (July 1974): 417. Although this definition substitutes a list of some component parts of appraisal for a definition of the term, it nevertheless makes clear that disposition is based upon an analysis of the information, and various factors affecting the information, within records.
    Several alternate meanings for the term appraisal also exist. Appraisal can involve the evaluation of a document for its financial value, as in appraising a document for insurance. Documents can also be appraised for their artistic merit, such as a medieval illuminated manuscript, or their significance as a historical artifact suitable for museum display, such as the American colonies' Declaration of Independence from Britain.
4. Carol Couture and Jean-Yves Rousseau. *The Life of a Document: A Global Approach to Archives and Records Management* (Montreal: Vehicule Press, 1982, translated into English by David Homel and republished

1987): 169. The words *evaluation* and *selection* are used to describe this process.

5.   The comparative approach used in this study was also based on the pragmatic observation that most archives have not undertaken the kind of detailed financial analysis of their total resources that would make possible a strict, accounting-like comparison.

6.   Four test sites that had agreed to participate in the project were unable to honor their commitment. The J. Walter Thompson & Co. archives was closed by its parent firm and its staff released. Changing personnel made it impossible for the Roman Catholic Archdiocese of Detroit and the Utah State Archives to participate in the project, and eliminated the participation of the Chase Manhattan Bank archives in the full test phase of the project. The Lutheran Church of America Archives was forced to withdraw when the merger of three Lutheran denominations led to a decision to build a new archives building, forcing the staff to abandon regular duties in order to plan for the new facility. The limited participation of the archives of the Episcopal Church of Canada, located in Toronto, and the Alabama State Archives, helped to fill some of the void created by participants who were forced to suspend participation.

7.   Statistics were drawn from information available regarding 11 participating institutions. By way of comparison Paul Conway, "Perspective on Archival Resources: the 1985 Census of Archival Institutions," *American Archivist* 50 (Spring 1987): 174-191, reports that, nationwide, the average archives had 3.7 professional staff members, total holdings that measured 7,900 linear feet, and annually accommodated 1,417 research visits.

8.   A few test sites put aside particularly knotty selection problems or other material they thought would make interesting examples with the expressed intention of using it as a part of this project. Although the appraisal of such specially chosen material did often give particular insight into the process, putting aside a controlled type of material to standardize test results across institutions was not part of the test design.

3

The Value-of-Information Module

Evaluating information is a traditional archival activity. At least since World War II archivists have tried to explain the intellectual processes through which it is done. As a result, archivists developed a number of ideas about how information should be evaluated, which were reviewed in chapter 1. Although archivists have explored many facets of selection, the archival community has never agreed upon a taxonomy to create an overall understanding of the process. Module I, *Value of Information*, incorporated these explanations into a systematic view of the evaluation of information. Because many points were included, the module was broken down into a complex arrangement of parts. This arrangement represents a synthesis of archival thought about information evaluation, but not a consensus.

One purpose of this chapter is to examine the validity of the component parts of this module. Because archivists have not developed standard definitions for the concepts used in selection, nor even clarified the broad generalizations, we must examine the terminology, as well as the potential intellectual pitfalls that exist in the concepts that underlie the terminology. Although discussing terminology is tedious, this preliminary discussion is essential to establish a consistently understood framework within which selection criteria can be intelligently discussed.

The second purpose of this chapter is to draw general conclusions regarding the importance placed by practicing archivists on the various evaluative ideas that have been defined. Although archivists have created numerous ideas about selection, they have never ascertained the relative importance of these concepts. The test data gathered from

participating archivists is used in an attempt to determine the importance of individual criteria in the day-to-day selection work of archivists.

As discussed in chapter 2, information evaluation is divided into four
clusters, each representing a major aspect of archival information
assessment. The clusters consist of:

- Functional characteristics
- Content analysis
- Relationship to other documentation
- Use.

This chapter is organized according to these clusters because it is a
useful way to conceptualize the process, but it is not without limitations.
Although the clusters are generally clear and distinct, they are not
rigidly separate; occasionally concepts and specific criteria overlap. To
cope with such problems, arbitrary distinctions between clusters are
sometimes imposed.

FIGURE 3-1. Functional Characteristics Cluster—Original Configuration

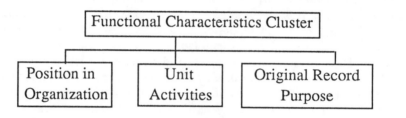

FUNCTIONAL CHARACTERISTICS

The concept of functional characteristics has been a part of archival
information analysis for over 20 years. Functional characteristics were
employed by Theodore Schellenberg to determine who made the records
and the purpose the records served for their creator.[1] Underlying this
analysis was the belief that important people or offices created records
that contain important information that would continue to be important
in the future.

The functional characteristics cluster was composed of three elements. The first element, creator's position in the organization, asked
how important the creator was in the official structure of the organization from which the records originated. The second element, unit activities, asked how significant the unit's role or responsibility was in the
originating institution. The third element, original function of the
record, asked how directly the records being evaluated were linked to
the unit function of the creating body.

Although the basic elements of functional characteristics have remained unchanged from Schellenberg's day, the passage of time has enhanced archival understanding of the elements and led to several significant revisions.

Functional Characteristics: Reinterpretation

Institutional archivists and manuscript archivists displayed divergent points of view after examining the functional characteristics cluster. For institutional archivists two relatively minor problems emerged. The first was a problem in assessing the comparative importance of the position in organization and unit function elements. The second problem was the relationship between the unit function and the original record function element.

Both the position in organization and unit function elements compared information about the record creator against a standard. The importance of a particular office was determined by examining the parent institution's organizational structure while the activities of an office were compared to the parent organization's activities. Although in theory these comparisons appeared to be clear, in practice the exact point of comparison proved uncertain, creating different evaluations of similar or identical records. For example, in one state archives two archivists evaluated identical records retained from the same state office, but rated that office's position and unit function very differently. Although personal differences accounted for some of this dissimilarity, a fuller explanation was that the two archivists compared the office and unit function to different levels in the state government. One archivist compared the office to the entire state government structure while the other thought in terms of the smaller, functional unit of state government in which the office was housed. Once this referential problem was recognized, arbitrarily imposing uniform evaluative reference points was relatively simple.

A more fundamental evaluative problem existed in the "original record purpose" element. As the element was conceived, an assumption was made that the closer the linkage between the record's original purpose and unit's primary activity, the more significant the information. This premise was established by thinking about record creation in high level, policy-making offices. In that situation, the premise assured that records linked to policy making would be considered important while records not linked to policy making would be considered unimportant.[2] Although the element had the expected result when records created by senior organizational officials were evaluated, when applied to low level offices the element created an unwanted result. If a unit's function was viewed as unimportant, for example an office regulating automobile parking, consistent application of the element's premise nevertheless meant that records closely linked to the unit's principal activity, such as issuing employee parking permits, would be evaluated as important. Test archivists firmly stated that parking permits and similar facilitative documents were not important archival records and suggested the need to modify the evaluative element's result.

One way to change the result was to redefine the element's standard of comparison. Rather than comparing record function to unit function, a more appropriate comparison was between record function and the overall goals and activities of the total organization. Using this standard, important policy documents would remain important, wherever they might be found, whereas parking permits, however central they were to the mission of the office creating them, would not be considered important.[3]

Although discussions with institutional archivists made it clear that some of the premises of the functional characteristics cluster needed modification, the comments of manuscript archivists were more radical, questioning the cluster's overall usefulness in evaluating manuscript records. Personal manuscripts or artificial collections gathered by collectors were difficult to place in an appropriate evaluative context. For example, how could an archivist evaluate the hierarchical position, the unit function, or the record function of letters written home by a soldier fighting in the Civil War? Viewed in the framework of manuscript archivists' collecting policies, the institutionally anchored context of the functional characteristics elements seemed irrelevant.

Some manuscript curators attempted to salvage the functional characteristics cluster by adopting the context of the questions to their institutional environment. Manuscript archivists often found that the document's original context was unrelated to the reasons they desired the documents. Curators using the functional characteristics cluster usually attempted to evaluate the documents according to some aspect of scholarly research rather than adopting a standard contemporary to the material. Scholarly interest, however, could often cover a wide variety of possible uses. Were a Civil War soldier's letters home to be judged against the context of the entire war's history, the history of a single campaign, the history of a particular regiment, a personal biography, or the demographic characteristics of men representing a particular region, economic strata, or educational background? The problem of developing a standard evaluative reference point for functional characteristics in a noninstitutional environment proved intractable and suggests that the cluster may have limited or no applicability in a manuscripts environment.

Although participating archivists initially thought that functional characteristics were well understood, during the course of the project these characteristics offered surprising challenges in establishing consistent standard of comparisons. Institutional archivists could answer these challenges by arbitrarily defining consistent, institution-based standards to judge the character of records created in that institution. Manuscript archivists, lacking an institutionally based reference point from which to judge the records, faced extremely difficult challenges in determining a useful comparative context for functional characteristics.

FIGURE 3-2.   Content Analysis Cluster—Original Configuration

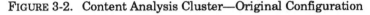

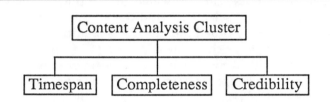

CONTENT ANALYSIS

The content analysis cluster examined records without regard to the purposes for which they were originally created in order to determine if they contained information relating to particular topics. At its simplest, content analysis consisted of reading the documents and deciding if the information in them was considered by the archivist to merit retention. Because records can and often do contain information on several subjects, the individual elements of the cluster could be reused for each topic the records addressed. Although records could potentially address an endless number of subjects, to establish some practical limit the word *significant* was stressed, and participating archivists were asked to identify no more than three specific topics. In its original configuration, three elements gauged content analysis: timespan, completeness, and credibility. Timespan was defined as a comparative measure between the time period covered by the records and the chronological period of the subject. Completeness asked how thoroughly the records documented the subject. Credibility asked if the information contained in the records was reliable.

Content Analysis: Reinterpretation

The archivists who worked with the content analysis cluster expressed a fundamental intellectual dissatisfaction with it. Although systematically articulating how an archivist analyzes record content had proved difficult for all those involved in the project, it was possible to improve the original cluster's intellectual structure. A better explanation of how an archivist undertakes content analysis should begin by linking a specific archive's mission statement, collecting policies, and other policies relevant to the content analysis of specific records. By using the archives' policies as a touchstone, archivists could then compare what was found in the records with the archives' acquisition goals or legal/administrative mandate. Using this procedure, records' content was evaluated through their relationship to the archives' goals.

Focusing content analysis through the lens of collecting policy follows logically from the archival literature written in the past decade,[4] but it is not clear that archivists widely accept the implicit restrictions this premise places on selection. Traditionally, archivists have considered content in a very broad manner. This tradition is best captured, and may spring from, Schellenberg's concept of informational value, which examines record content in the broadest possible way.[5] Closely linking collecting policy to selection means, however, that in most cases only a narrow set of records will be accepted by a particular archival institution. Records whose content causes them to fall outside that set will be rejected regardless of their potential value. Although easy to support in the abstract, the number of archives that continue to operate without clear mandates and collecting foci, and the inability of some archivists to reject "good stuff" that is beyond the scope of their institutional collecting policy, suggests that the need for, and the consequences of, a narrow content focus may not be fully accepted by all archivists.

Despite this potential criticism, linking archival collecting policy to the content analysis of specific records was a critical improvement in the intellectual structure of the cluster, but further refinement of the elements was also needed. The three elements originally presented failed to capture significant analytical points. As a result of many participants' suggestions, the cluster was reconfigured to include five evaluative elements:

- Significance of topic
- Timespan
- Completeness
- Credibility
- Creator's relationship to topic.

Of the revised cluster's five elements, participants identified three as particularly important: significance of the topic, timespan, and completeness. The more closely the basic topics of a particular set of records coincide with the core collection or the core collecting goals of a particular archival institution, the more valuable the material is to that archives.[6]

FIGURE 3-3. Content Analysis Cluster—Revised Configuration

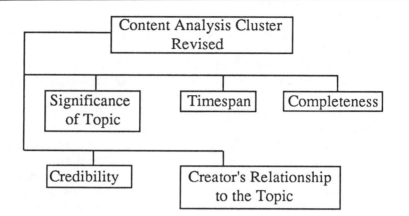

The concept underlying timespan is straightforward. Timespan compares the time period covered by the records to the relevant chronological period of the subject. For example, the chronological period covered by the papers of a nineteenth-century settler might be compared to the dates of the pioneer period of the local community. Although understanding the concept of timespan is simple, actually using it to select records requires resolving two questions: What is the appropriate comparative timespan? How does one assess the chronological coverage of a particular set of records?

The timespan of a subject can be conceptualized in two ways. The first method is to use accepted and sometimes arbitrary dates that define an event or period. These dates may be established by the event itself, or, in other cases, a time frame may be established through the research of scholars or other interested parties. For example, an event like the Detroit Race Riot of June 20-22, 1943, defines its own timespan. Thoughtfully characterizing periods of race relations in Detroit during the twentieth century, however, is likely to depend on scholarly endeavor. A more complex way to conceptualize timespan is to focus on the period of time most critical for the topic. In discussing race relations in Detroit, a critical moment in racial harmony occurred between 1939 and 1941 when black workers were successfully integrated into the primarily white membership of the emerging United Automobile Workers union. A critical period of disunity might be represented by the abandonment of the core city by the white middle class in the years following Detroit's 1967 race riot. Self-defining timespans or timespans that cover a number of years are usually more objective than timespans defined by judgment regarding "critical" periods or moments of history. Focusing upon critical moments, however, can develop a body of documentation that is of maximum research interest. Deciding how to implement the timespan element is difficult since each way of conceptualizing it offers advantages and disadvantages. Where critical historical moments can be agreed upon, they would appear to be the preferred conceptual framework for this element.

A second problem regarding timespan involved determining the chronological coverage of records. Archivists report the chronological span of records in two ways. Cataloging rules use span dates, which report the earliest date and latest date in a given set of records, but most archivists also discuss bulk dates, an often inexact period into which a large majority of records fall. The difference between span and bulk dates is one of record distribution. Span dates often misrepresent a collection because using two outlying records fails to note significant chronological gaps between the span dates. Unlike people who were born in 1911, died in 1989, and presumably filled up the years in between with more or less equal amounts of work, records existing between 1911 and 1989 may lack documents for periods of months, years, or even decades. However, even bulk dates may not reveal uneven chronological distributions in a particular set of records. There is no simple way to resolve how archivists should evaluate the chronological coverage of a given set of records. Bulk dates are probably of more analytical value than span dates, and uneven distribution of records or chronological gaps in record sets needs to be weighed against the specific dates being sought.[7]

The third major element in the content cluster, completeness, evaluates how thoroughly the records document a subject. Although logic suggests that completeness should be subjected to the same, or more rigorous, analysis that was applied to timespan, the concept of completeness was used by archivists with little trouble or comment. It would be comforting to believe that the easy acceptance of completeness indicates that archivists understood this element. The difficulty experienced by archivists in *defining* completeness, however, suggests that the underlying concepts were not sufficiently clear to allow thorough analysis. The term *completeness* itself may be an umbrella concept that covers a number of unarticulated assumptions that may in the future be divided into two or more elements.

Significance of topic, timespan, and completeness are the three major elements of the content analysis cluster, but two other infrequently applied elements can also affect the cluster: *credibility/authenticity*, which addresses the reliability of the information, and *creator's relationship to the topic*, which defines the link between the information and the person supplying it. These two elements rarely play roles in selection because in most cases archivists assume that they are present. In general, archival materials are credible and authentic and are created by individuals who were participants in or observers of the events and issues being described. The elements of credibility/authenticity and the creator's relationship to the topic affect very few selection decisions, usually in a negative way. Inauthentic records or records describing topics of which the author had no real knowledge were not likely to be preserved.

In summary, the content analysis cluster presented more intellectual challenges and left more unanswered questions than any other part of the information module. By linking collecting policy to topic, and using five elements, of which significance of topic, timespan, and completeness are most important, a clearer explanation of the cluster was created. This current explanation of how archivists evaluate content, however, has important shortcomings. Repeatedly, archivists involved in the project expressed concern that "something was missing" in the cluster, yet no insight emerged to define the missing element(s). The manner in which archivists evaluate record content is not well understood and is a strong candidate for future research.

RELATIONSHIP TO OTHER DOCUMENTATION

The third cluster of ideas participating archivists used to evaluate information involved comparisons between the documents being examined and other records or information. Comparisons were made in two ways. The first comparison was a physical matching of the records at hand with other records known to exist. The second comparison matched the information in the records at hand with other information.[8] Acknowledging this division, the *relationship to other records* cluster was divided into two subclusters: *physical qualities* and *intellectual content*. Each subcluster will be discussed separately.

FIGURE 3-4.   Relationship to Other Documentation: Physical Qualities Subcluster—Original Configuration

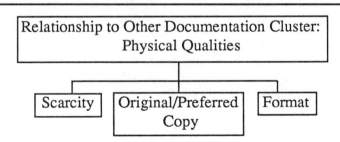

Physical qualities compared three physical characteristics of records: scarcity, original/preferred copy, and format. Scarcity was an indicator of how common were records of a similar genre to the ones

being examined. Original/preferred copy asked if this were the most desirable version of the records. Format asked the desirability of the records physical arrangement and type.

Physical Qualities: Reinterpretation

Although the proposed elements captured some of the ideas that archivists employed, the subcluster did not completely describe how archivists thought about this problem. Further analysis led to a reconceptualization of the physical characteristics subcluster into four elements: scarcity, organization, original/preferred copy, and format. Of these, the first two elements are the more important.

FIGURE 3-5.   Relationship to Other Documentation: Physical Qualities Subcluster—Revised Configuration

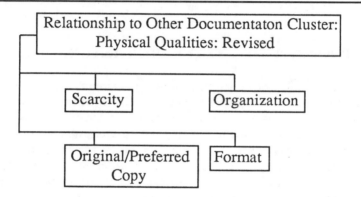

Although virtually every archivist in the project considered scarce records to be archivally important, how the archivists defined scarce, or more correctly, how they established an appropriate comparative context, differed from person to person. Four ways of defining scarcity were proposed:

- The age of the document
- The document's general rarity
- The document's rarity in relationship to a particular topic
- A document's rarity in a particular repository.

Some archivists argued that all old documents should be saved. Other archivists argued that scarcity, not age itself, was the truly important factor. For example, thousands of diaries written during the nineteenth century survive today, making them a relatively common genre of documents, but in the latter half of the twentieth century diary-keeping has become a lost art, making a diary written in the 1970s a genuinely scarce item. Scarcity is, however, a relatively vague measure, and therefore other archivists wished to link scarcity to either a particular topic or the holdings of a particular institution. Thus, an appropriate comparative reference might be not all nineteenth century diaries, but nineteenth-century diaries that detail women's activities in pioneer communities.

The question of scarcity's comparative context is important because the context directly affects what records are deemed important. Although an argument can be made for any of the four contexts mentioned, the preferable way to define scarcity is in relationship to a particular archive's institutional collecting policy. In this way, scarcity is directly linked to the mission and goals of a particular institution, rather than becoming a free-floating element that can be used to justify any selection decision. To simply save "old things" because they are old transforms rational archival policies into antiquarianism. Although items that are rare in society generally might merit preservation somewhere, to expect archival selectors to understand the entire spectrum of records places an overwhelming burden on them. To expect institutions to accept responsibility for rare items that do not fall within their collecting scope or bureaucratic mandate is to ask parent institutions to fund archives that have no sharply defined focus. Saving scarce material would eventually cause an archival collection to degenerate into a randomly selected group of records gathered through the impressionistic attitudes of the archives' staff. Scarcity, ultimately, should be defined through an institutional policy established by the archives which clarifies within the framework of the archives' mission and goals what kinds of records are "scarce."

The second element in the subcluster, the organization of information, was not originally included in the model, but several archivists' comments made clear that it was an important part of information evaluation. Information that is well organized and easily accessible is of greater use than the same information presented in a disordered and inaccessible way. These positive qualities enhance the value of even mediocre information. It is because of information organization that a thorough and well-indexed newspaper clipping file discussing a political campaign is often more used than a rich but poorly organized set of records created by the campaign manager.

In comparison to scarcity and organization, the elements of original/preferred copy and format play a minor role in selection and in most cases are irrelevant. The only known copy of a set of records is by default the original or the preferred copy. Similarly, when records are available in only one format, primarily paper in most archives, the question of format becomes irrelevant. These elements are applicable primarily in archives dealing with the records of large institutions where multiple paper copies are created, copies are distributed in different formats, or copies are generated from computerized files. In such a setting an archivist may well have to weigh where the original copy of a record should be located and select from a number of different physical formats.

FIGURE 3-6.   Relationship to Other Documentation: Intellectual Qualities Cluster—Original Configuration

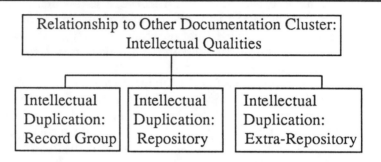

Intellectual Qualities

Intellectual qualities was the second subcluster of the relationship to other documentation cluster. Intellectual qualities assessed the information duplication of records in three contexts. The elements asked if the information in the records was available in the record group or collection itself; in the archival repository in which the records would be retained; or in the universe of information that exists outside the repository.

Although the three elements that made up intellectual duplication were easily understood, problems complicated their application. As with so many other elements, the most interesting problem revolved around the context in which the archivist made these comparisons. When comparing the information found in a particular set of records to the information in a repository, there are two ways to construe repository holdings: either as records already accessioned by the repository or as anticipated archival accessions. Records that appear unique when judged against the conservative standard of what is actually on the archives' shelves may prove highly duplicative when measured against the more liberal standard of what the archives should or hopes to receive. Deciding what constitutes *repository holdings* is a risk-taking exercise based on an archivist's experience with and future expectations of records management and field collecting programs. If past experiences have been good and future expectations of regular and predictable accessions are high, then it is reasonable to compare the records being evaluated against not only current holdings but also future accessions.

If past experiences or future expectations regarding regular and pre-dictable accessions are poor, then limiting the comparison to current holdings is both safer and more logical.

At the extra-repository level a significant practical difficulty exists in determining the content of the comparative information universe. The theoretical importance of this activity has been persuasively argued.[9] Practically, however, it is difficult to discover what information is actually available outside the archivist's own institution. There is no simple, systematic way by which definitive, detailed information can be obtained regarding the content of other local, regional, or national information centers. Discovering information "out there" is, in practice, a vexing problem.[10]

Beyond questions of context, the impact of intellectual duplication must take into account the inherent importance of interrelated informa-tion in an archives. Although it is a truism that archives seek and preserve information that is unique, one of the most important virtues of a well-integrated archival collection is not the absolute uniqueness of the records but rather the web of interrelated information that is created by a focused archival collecting policy. Collecting focus makes it possible for a researcher to research a particular question using sources that reflect differing perspectives. For example, the papers of one Italian immigrant may be interesting, but the collected material of many immigrants and immigrant organizations, including personal accounts, relevant fraternal organizational records, documents from ethnic churches and schools, and ethnic newspaper files, assume a collective importance for ethnic history greater than the individual parts. Simi-larly, in a particular record group, two sets of related information may make possible a more accurate representation of the past than either set individually.

The inescapable conclusion to be drawn from this analysis is that the preservation of unique information is not equally important at each of the three comparative levels of this subcluster, and often is not the most important institutional goal for an archives. At the record group and the repository level, the appropriate institutional goal may be to seek complementary, rather than unique, information. The balance between complementary and unique information may well be decided by the institutional goals of the particular archives. Those archives seeking to strengthen already existing bodies of information will natu-rally seek complementary records, while institutions seeking to estab-lish themselves over a broad area of intellectual concerns, or seeking to move in new directions, may chose to emphasize uniqueness.

The elements in the *relationship to other documents* cluster are important evaluative tools. Physical comparisons, based particularly on scarcity and organization of records, are of great importance in the evaluation of information. Intellectual comparisons among the records being evaluated, with other records in the repository, and with information available in the broadest possible sense, are also significant.

USE CLUSTER

The final cluster of elements employed to evaluate information is *use*. Perhaps the most controversial of the clusters incorporated into the *value of information* module, *use* reflects the belief that information that is not used is not worth retention.[11] The use cluster was divided into two subclusters: user interest and use limitations.

FIGURE 3-7. Use—User Interest Subcluster—Original Configuration

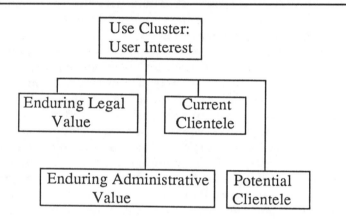

User Interest

The first subcluster involved use of the records both by those who created them and by other interested parties who may use them for a variety of reasons. The probability that those who created the records will want to use them in the future is often evaluated through two elements derived from records management: *enduring legal* and *enduring administrative* values. Use by other individuals, often called secondary record users, can be evaluated through two other elements: use by the archives current research clientele, and potential use of the records by other known user groups.

Although the elements of enduring legal and enduring administrative functions are clearly defined concepts, there is one troubling issue regarding their scope. As usually presented, the legal and administrative needs discussed are those of the records' creator. It is possible, however, to think of occasions in which the legal position of a litigant is documented in the records of others. Furthermore, in some cases, the litigant will initiate a suit that is detrimental to the records' creator, and use court-ordered discovery proceedings to explore the records creator's files for incriminating documentation. In civil proceedings the plaintiff's ability to prove a claim may ultimately rest on records created by the corporation or person being sued. Similarly, the claims of individuals or groups against government agencies may require documentation from those agencies in order to validate the claim.

The possibility of third parties using records for legal purposes unrelated or even detrimental to the records' creator raises philosophical issues regarding an archives obligation to maintain records of legal value to those who did not create them. The records management literature has suggested that the legal value of documentation should be evaluated exclusively in terms of its potential to help or harm the record creator.[12] Since records managers generally define their responsibilities in terms of their employer's best interest, this position is logically consistent with their professional goals.

Archivists, however, frequently define their responsibilities in broad social terms and include in their professional objectives goals that transcend the immediate objectives of the records' creator. In most cases, this transcendent mission to society complements and supplements the goals of the parent organization or the donor. It is in instances where the retention of records may cause legal harm to the institution creating the records or to the donor that a difficult question concerning the archivist's professional responsibility is raised. This ethical problem does not lend itself to easy resolution and suggests the need for a thoughtful discussion among archivists over the ethical balance to be struck between responsibility to one's employer or donors and the profession's societal mission.[13]

The elements of actual and potential clientele use needed refinement. As a minor clarification, consideration of the potential clientele element should not be interpreted as an exercise in archival prophecy. The element's comparative universe was known researchers in other archives who do not visit the selecting institution. Because archivists lack any interinstitutional reporting tool discussing use, it is a problem to discover who visits other institutions. Even after this severe handicap is acknowledged, discovering information about researchers in other archives is a far more realistic goal than attempting to predict future research trends.

A more important clarification about clientele involves the ranking of users in order of importance. Although some archivists consider all users equally important, other archivists prioritize user groups. An academic archives, for example, may be mandated to serve faculty and other advanced researchers, and thus may logically give preference to records particularly important to their needs. A public library may be mandated to serve the citizens of a particular area, and thus the library's special collections unit may give preference to the records that the largest number of their patrons, probably genealogists, find important. Where user groups are prioritized, it is reasonable to ask if the information being evaluated would serve the actual or potential clientele(s) that the archives considers important.[14]

FIGURE 3-8. Use—User Limitation Subcluster—Original Configuration

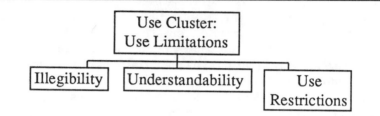

Use Limitations

The second subcluster in the use cluster was *use limitations. Limitations* consists of three elements:

- Illegibility—the inability of anyone to actually read the written characters.
- Understandability—the ability to comprehend what it is the abstract symbols on the medium mean.
- Access restrictions—which determine who may see the records and under what conditions.

The three elements in the use limitations subcluster proved the most stable of all the parts of the information module. No archivist questioned illegibility. Understandability was also generally accepted, although a question was raised regarding who needed to understand the records. An institution with ethnic holdings, for example, constantly discovered records that are not understandable to English-speaking archivists because they were written in the native tongue of the immigrant. Scientific records such as the research notebooks documenting laboratory experiments can present the same kind of problem to individuals not conversant in the discipline. To destroy such records because they are incomprehensible to the archivist is unwarranted. Rather, the appropriate comparative standard for understandability was the level of knowledge possessed by a person conversant in the field or language under consideration.

In considering the element of access restrictions, the concept of ranking users proved important. A particularly striking example of this was seen in the use of closed business archives. Business archives have been criticized because they often are not open to the general public. A business archivist, however, can adopt the position that although this is true, the corporate records are open to the users the archives were established to serve, officers and staff of the corporation itself. Since these primary users have complete access to the archives' materials, a business archivist can argue that by a practical definition of use, the corporation's archives are open. The connection business archivists can draw between the archives' primary audience, that audience's access to the records, and use, is similar to the policies of many research-oriented archives that have accepted collections open only to "serious research-ers." Indeed, business archivists may be on firmer ground than research-oriented archivists, since access based on corporate affiliation is clear, while access based on the seriousness of the applicant is open to wide variations in interpretation. Pragmatically, then, defining record closure in terms of the people for whom the archives is established to serve remains a traditional archival approach.

RELATIVE IMPORTANCE OF ELEMENTS AND CLUSTERS

Having discussed the intellectual issues affecting the clusters and elements of the *value of information* module, it is useful to determine the relative importance test-site participants placed on them. This can be done two ways. First, individual elements can be ranked to determine what specific record features archivists used most to evaluate information. Second, the 19 elements can be collapsed into seven groups, to draw some general conclusions about what qualities archivists seek when they evaluate information.

Individual Elements

The mosaic formed by examining the rank order of individual elements in the information module reveals two general images. First, archivists differentiate between the elements in the module in terms of their overall importance. Second, this differentiation may result from a preference for objective rather than subjective elements. Both of these findings have important implications.

Differentiation between module elements among archivists is conceptually important. In discussing selection, the archival literature has historically presented selection elements in a flat, nonprioritized manner. Archivists have been offered a large number of elements that may affect selection, but those offering these elements failed to advise archivists regarding which elements were most significant. This project suggests that even without such "expert" advice, practicing archivists have made decisions on the significance of various selection elements. In the future, selection theory should take into account and explain this observed prioritization of selection elements.

TABLE 3-1. Rank Order of Individual Value-of-Information Elements[15]

	Element	Average Score
1	Scarcity	3.46
2	Unit Activity	3.15
3	Comparison - Rep. Level	3.00
4	Administrative Use	2.92
4	Hierarchy	2.92
6	Secondary Users - actual	2.69
6	Legal Use	2.69
6	Record Function	2.69
9	Completeness	2.62
10	Secondary Users - pot.	2.46
10	Comparison - RG Level	2.46
12	Credibility	2.23
12	Illegibility	2.23
14	Access Restrictions	2.16
15	Comparison - Extra-rep.	2.08
15	Understandability	2.08
17	Original/Prefer. Copy	2.00
18	Timespan	1.92
19	Format	1.85

The second observation that can be drawn from the rank order of elements is that the elements seem to fall into several groups which are of descending levels of importance. In general these groups move from the concrete to the abstract, although exceptions to this pattern exist. The element most often looked at in selection is scarcity. Second, archivists ask questions regarding the activity of the unit. Third, archivists ask questions about three elements: where the creator is placed in the administrative hierarchy of the organization, if there will be any subsequent administrative use, and if similar materials are already in the archives. Fourth, archivists think about the elements of secondary users, potential legal importance, the record's original function, and the completeness of the documentation. Fifth are the elements of potential use by secondary users and comparison in the record group itself. These 11 elements seem to be the most important in the evaluation of information. The remaining eight elements have very little impact upon most record evaluations. Credibility, illegibility, access restrictions, comparisons with records outside the archives, understandability, the original/preferred copy, timespan, and format, are all usually relegated by archivists to a minor role.[16]

When archivists consider the rank order of the first 11 elements they base them on a continuum that moves from the objective to the subjective. The exact placement on that continuum appears to be affected by the ease or difficulty with which the archivist can obtain the information necessary to substantiate a conclusion. Scarcity and unit activity, the two highest ranked elements, can both be determined with relative objectivity. Whatever their definition of scarcity, archivists believe they have a good idea of what documents fall into that category. Similarly, discovering what a unit does is a fairly straightforward task. In the case of both elements, information is objective and comparatively simple to obtain. Comparisons with other information contained in the repository, potential administrative use, and position in hierarchy are also elements for which straightforward questions can be answered in a reasonably definitive manner.

As the archivist moves along the continuum, however, the questions become more subjective and the answers become more speculative. Determining the interest of existing archives patrons in a particular record group often involves some guesswork. Determining potential legal use is also often speculative. Completeness can be a difficult question to gauge and determining original record function can become a time-consuming task, sometimes requiring information that is difficult to obtain. Similarly, the final group of important elements represents very speculative judgments. Predicting the likelihood that records will attract new users to the archives, or examining records for duplication at the record group level can be difficult and very time-consuming. Although this examination of the ranking assigned to these elements is obviously incomplete, it does offer a broad interpretation of the research data.

Clusters

Looking at individual elements is instructive, but it can be frustrating when the wealth of detail obscures generalizations. To facilitate a broader view, the 19 elements were collapsed into seven element groups, usually ranked by archivists in the following order of importance shown in Table 3-2:

TABLE 3-2. Rank Order of Collapsed Value-of-Information Elements

Collapsed Elements	Average Score
1 Functional Analysis	2.92
2 Records Management	2.80
3 Users	2.58
4 Intellectual Duplication	2.51
5 Physical Duplication	2.44
6 Content	2.26
7 Use limits	2.16

This cluster order reinforces the general project conclusion that archivists evaluate information based on a continuum that moves from objective, simple-to-implement clusters to subjective, difficult-to-implement clusters. As with the elements, the element groups fall into interpretive categories. Functional characteristics, dominated by two easily answered questions— who made the records, and what was their position in the organization—ranked first, closely followed by the equally direct records management cluster. The middle categories of users, intellectual duplication, and physical duplication, represent data that is more difficult to gather but which contains some elements that are relatively objective and relatively simple to use. The final two groupings—content and use limits—do not fit as nicely into the overall interpretive framework presented here. Content evaluation is obviously among the most difficult of clusters to employ, and represents some of the most subjective judgments made by archivists. Use limits, on the other hand, are fairly straightforward. The low ranking use limits received probably indicates that it, like the other poorly ranked elements already discussed, was considered inconsequential to most selection decisions.

FIGURE 3-9. Value-of-Information Module—Revised Configuration

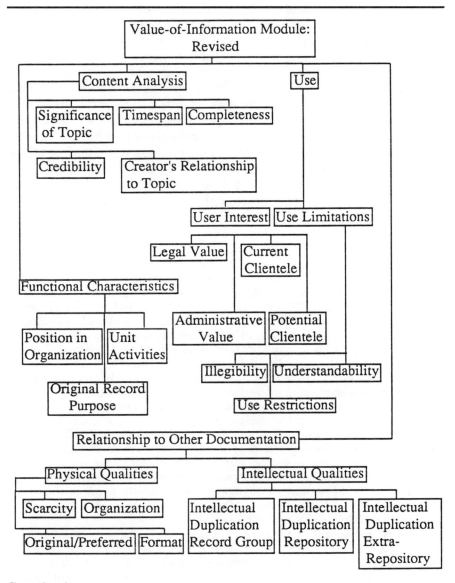

Conclusion

Archivists have devoted more thought to the information module than to any other aspect of the selection process. That effort has resulted in the complex array of elements which make up the module. Research data gathered through this study lead to four major findings. First, the elements used in this study to explain selection appear by and large to be what archivists consider when they make decisions regarding information selection. Second, although the general outlines of archival information selection appear clear, archival practice has not created uniform criteria which capture how information is evaluated for archival purposes. Third, even for those elements that are commonly agreed upon, specific definitions do not exist, leading to idiosyncratic personal and institutional practices. Fourth, archivists do not attach equal importance to each of the information module's elements. Instead they have established a continuum of importance basing the significance of the element upon the two principles of objectivity and ease of application. In summary, while archivists have agreed to a broad outline of how to evaluate information and are moving toward a more detailed understanding of the elements of that outline, they have not yet fully articulated the criteria or the process through which the criteria are implemented.

Endnotes

1. Theodore R. Schellenberg, "The Appraisal of Modern Public Records," National Archives Bulletin #8 (Washington: National Archives and Records Service, 1956), as reprinted in *A Modern Archives Reader: Basic Readings on Archival Theory and Practice*, Maygene Daniels and Timothy Walch, eds., (Washington: National Archives and Records Service, 1984): 57-70. In Schellenberg's terminology these were "evidential values." Specifically regarding the continuing historical importance of significant administrative records, Schellenberg wrote, "In applying the test of evidential value the archivist is likely to preserve records that have other values as well—records that are useful not only for the public administrator and the students of public administration, but also for the economist, sociologist, historian, and scholars generally." Ibid., 60.

2. This stress on the importance of identifying documents discussing policy making was based on an uncritical acceptance of Schellenberg's pyramid model of records, which stressed the importance of documents created by those few offices that sat atop a bureaucratic pyramid of agencies. See *Modern Archives: Principles and Techniques* (Chicago: University of Chicago Press, 1956): 143-144.

3. Another potential way to make this judgment would be to evaluate documents through record form. David Bearman and Richard Lytle have argued for the importance of form as an indicator of content. This project, however, did not attempt to test the practical implications of Bearman and Lytle's thesis. See Bearman and Lytle, "The Power of the Principle of Provenance," *Archivaria* 21 (Winter 1985/86): 14-27.

4. See particularly Jutta Reed-Scott, "Collection Management Strategies for Archivists," *American Archivist* 47 (1984):23-29; Faye Phillips, "Developing Collecting Policies for Manuscript Collections," *American Archivist* 47 (1984):30-42; Helen Samuels, "Who Controls the Past," *American Archivist* 49 (1986):109-124; and Frank Boles, "Mix Two Parts Interest to One Part Information and Appraise Until Done: Understanding Con-

temporary Record Selection," *American Archivist* 50 (Summer 1987): 356-369.

5. Theodore R. Schellenberg, *Modern Archives,* 148-160.

6. Because collecting policies and other policy documents are usually vague, in many cases institutional precedent will serve to define core collecting areas. Whether defined consciously through policy or unconsciously through years of precedent, specific topics will come to be regarded as core, supplemental, peripheral, or out-of-scope. Judith Endelman, "Looking Backward to Plan for the Future: Collection Analysis for Manuscript Repositories," offers several insights into both how archives accumulate records on a variety of topics and how precedent can be used to consciously help establish policies that prioritize among those topics.

7. Archivists responsible for the selection of a specific set of records could employ a sampling scheme to render an impartial statement regarding the distribution of a particular set of documents through time. However, the implementation of such a scheme would prove time-consuming and in order to be meaningful would require more basic research to develop a "normal" chronological distribution of records to serve as a comparative standard. Archivists could attempt to bypass research by developing a consensus based on intuitive knowledge, but it would be open to endless discussion and criticism.

8. Joan K. Haas, Helen Willa Samuels, and Barbara Trippel Simmons, *Appraising the Records of Modern Science and Technology: A Guide* (Boston: Massachusetts Institute of Technology, 1985): 9. This document makes a far-reaching statement regarding the importance of information comparison.

9. Ibid.

10. *Information centers* is used in this work as a generic term that includes archives, libraries, electronic databases, and other relevant institutions or sources that possess documentation related to the information included within the records being evaluated. Although archivists interested in discovering what is "out there" may refer to traditional tools such as the National Union Catalog of Manuscripts, or online databases such as that maintained by the Research Library Information Network, the lack of systematic authority control and the brief descriptions found in such sources only highlight the difficulties that hinder interinstitutional archival information exchange.

11. Lawrence Dowler, "The Role of Use in Defining Archival Practice and Principles: A Research Agenda for the Availability and Use of Records," *American Archivist* 51 (1988): 74-86.

12. David O. Stephens, "Making Records Retention Decisions: Practical and Theoretical Considerations," *Records Management Quarterly* 22 (January 1988): 3-7.

13. This legal concern is not completely theoretical. In the case of *American Friends Service Committee* v. *Webster*, more commonly known to archivists as the FBI records appraisal case, plaintiffs argued that the retention schedules originally established by the National Archives failed to take into consideration the legal rights of those who may have been harmed by an FBI action. Plaintiffs argued that the schedules should have included consideration of the need to preserve records in order for

individual citizens to document alleged violation of law by the FBI through relevant FBI files. Although in this particular case the philosophical issue could be decided by determining to whom the National Archives is primarily responsible, the federal bureaucracy or the nation's citizens, broadly considered it is an example of outsiders hoping to use records created by a bureaucracy to demonstrate that the bureaucracy had harmed them. On the corporate level one can easily imagine environmentalists bringing suit against various corporations and using discovery proceedings in an effort to locate records demonstrating willful corporate disregard for specific statutes or the general public good.

14. This prioritization is usually done subtly and does not involve conscious decisions by reference staff to be more "helpful" to one class of patrons over another. Commonly it involves acquisition, arrangement, and descriptive decisions that highlight information of use to one group while giving a lesser priority to information useful to others. For example, academic archives frequently underdescribe material of genealogical interest, whereas special collection units in public libraries often develop extensive genealogical research tools but cannot find staff time to describe in detail records of value to "serious" historians.

The prioritization of users also raises the question of whether archivists, as a class, should be considered a distinct user population of archival material. If Michael Cook and Susan Steinwall's previously cited argument that archivists have overstressed the concept of evidential value because of distinctly archival needs is accepted, at a minimum it means that institutional archivists have, de facto, prioritized material necessary for their own descriptive work. By extension archivists might also choose to prioritize certain items because the documents simplify reference. The archivist as document user, with distinct professional interests and needs, is an area worthy of study.

15. Analysis of the prioritization placed on elements in this and in other clusters is based on numbers derived from participants weighting of the elements. Each of the 19 elements within the *value of information* module were ranked on a one to four scale by participating archivists, four being the highest score, one the lowest. Because of the unscientific character of the sample and the very small sample size the differences in the average element scores are not statistically significant. The average scores are included because of the pioneering character of the information, however, the reader should approach them with the caution that a larger survey would probably change the absolute number and might also change the rank order of the elements.

16. Element groups presented here are based on two rationales. For the first 11 elements, distinctions were drawn based on the relative difference between average element scores. An element which demonstrated more than a 0.15 distance between itself and its predecessor was placed in a separate group. Groups of elements that had less than a 0.15 distance between them were lumped together. The final eight elements were grouped together and determined to be of minimal importance based on a comparison of their score and the highest average score found in the costs-of-information module (1.92). Archivists in the test group held costs to be a minor factor in selection, therefore it was logical to assume

that information module elements that had average scores in the same range as costs were also of relatively little influence. Although the highest scoring element in the group deemed unimportant had a score somewhat higher than the best score achieved with the costs module, nevertheless the pattern in this group, in which each element's score was relatively close to that of its successor, suggested that the elements should be treated as a unit.

4

The Costs-of-Retention and Implications-of-the-Selection Decision Modules

This chapter explores the response of archivists to the ideas contained in the *Costs of Retention* and *Implications of the Selection Decision* modules. Its structure is the same as chapter 3, first defining terms and ideas and then discussing the critique archivists made regarding the terms. Because both modules are based upon controversial theoretical assumptions about the nature of archival selection, not only are the component parts of the modules discussed, but the basic premises for including the module are also examined. The chapter concludes with a very brief discussion of the relative importance archivists placed on the three modules.

The rich layers of thought that are apparent when archivists discuss the *value of information* module are not present in the discussion of these two subsequent modules. Archivists have addressed the issues raised by these two modules in a summary fashion, perhaps because of the controversial assumptions imbedded in modules two and three. Reflecting the lack of archival analysis, the discussion of these two modules tends to be shorter and less detailed than the discussion of the *value of information* module.

COSTS-OF-RETENTION MODULE: INTRODUCTION

Retaining, arranging, describing, and referencing records involves costs. As was noted in chapter 1, archivists have argued for almost half a century over whether or not these costs should be incorporated into the selection decision. G. Philip Bauer, in 1944, argued that no sensible evaluation of records could avoid the issue of costs, but in the same publication Herman Kahn argued that taking costs into consideration was culturally unacceptable. The argument that Bauer and Kahn began almost 50 years ago remains unresolved today.

This section accepts Bauer's argument and examines the role costs play in evaluating potential archival acquisitions. As noted in chapter 2, costs are construed broadly and include five components:

- Acquisition
- Processing
- Conservation
- Storage
- Reference.

As in the preceding chapter, the principle goals are to create broadly acceptable definitions of costs, analyze the intellectual strengths and weakness of those definitions, and report on how the archivists who participated in this study actually used costs in selection.

FIGURE 4-1. Acquisition Costs Cluster

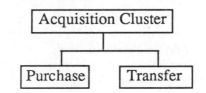

PURCHASE AND ACQUISITION

As originally configured this component consisted of two elements, purchase and acquisition. Although only a minority of archivists routinely purchase archival material, those who do must compare the information in the record with the price requested for the record(s).[1] The purpose of this comparison is to determine if the price asked is a fair one and if the archival institution either has, or can raise, the money.

The majority of archives receive new material through legislative mandate, administrative directives institutionalized through records management programs, or through the good will of individual donors. In all of the above examples the individual last possessing the records does not receive any financial compensation for the records transferred to the archives.[2] Although such records are "free," transferring the documents to the archives does involve costs. These costs can include:

the staff time and transportation costs incurred in sending an archivist to either evaluate a particular group of records where they are stored, or to write a retention and disposal schedule; the staff time and supply costs involved in preparing the records for shipment to the archives; and the direct costs of shipping the material to the archives.

Acquisition: Revisions

Because archivists who participated in the project rarely purchased archival material, the justifications underlying the purchase element were not examined. Although all of the archivists did incur transfer costs, the out-of-pocket expenses were usually minimal, and the time staff devoted to transferring material to the archives was rarely considered as an expense. Generally, archivists considered the costs associated with transferring material as a routine operating expense, like the bills for space, heat, or light. Because acquisition costs were treated as operating expenses they were usually not considered when a selection decision was made.

Acquisition costs played a role in selection only when archivists faced what they considered to be extraordinary costs. Archivists at several institutions, particularly repositories that collect private manuscripts, reconsidered their evaluation of the records information if the papers in question were considered a particularly large acquisition, contained large numbers of nontextual, or nonpaper records, or the archives had to pay to ship the material a substantial distance.

The way most archivists approached acquisition costs was indicative of the way archivists approach most cost considerations that could affect selection. Costs were usually treated as fixed, and ignored unless the character of the records under consideration was in some way atypical. Atypicality, whether of size, format, or some other concern, brought cost into the selection decision.

PROCESSING COSTS

The *processing costs* cluster was constructed of three elements: level of expertise, costs of supplies, and quantity of work. As initially organized, the cluster was based on the assumption that the archivist first considered the complexity of the processing tasks to be undertaken and the requisite level of archival expertise needed to successfully complete those tasks. Second, the costs of supplies was taken into consideration, particularly if the archives routinely reboxed or refoldered material. This cluster, however, differentiated between supply costs and costs attributable to preservation decisions. The distinction is seen in the price of a new banker's box, and the higher price for a new acid-free container of similar size. The cost of the banker's box is a supply cost, while the difference in price between the banker's box and the acid-free box is a preservation cost. Third, the quantity of work was considered to reflect the different amounts of time needed to process differing collections. Examples of problems that can affect processing time include the size of a group of records, the acceptability of the records' original order, the level of intellectual access sought, and the record formats found in the material.

FIGURE 4-2. Processing Costs Cluster

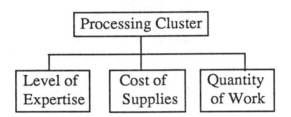

Underlying this three-element structure was the belief that most archives had either an established policy or long-standing customs regarding the appropriate level of processing required by a particular set of records. This policy or set of customs would serve as a reference point for the archivist when he or she applied the elements

Processing: Revisions

The definitions assigned to the three elements of processing costs oversimplified the processing options available to archivists. In particular, the level of expertise and the quantity of work elements could be interpreted by archivists in a wide variety of ways. The level of expertise element assumed that a single person with a specified skill level would process a given set of records. In reality, however, an archivist may determine that a variety of tasks will be undertaken to arrange and describe a single set of records and that different individuals will perform those tasks. Some tasks, such as determining the original order of a badly damaged filing system, may require the skill of a professional archivist. Other tasks, such as checking the alphabetical order of a topical file or placing a group of letters in chronological order, may be undertaken by a paraprofessional or clerical employee.

The quantity of work is dependent upon choices made by a processing archivist. A decision, for example, to accept without change a poorly organized topical file has implications very different from a decision to reorganize the same file. Similarly, a decision that the original folders housing material in a one hundred foot collection are good enough, thus avoiding the purchase of several thousand new folders, can drastically alter both the time needed to process a particular set of records as well as the cost of supplies.

The original configuration of the processing component failed to capture the flexibility most archivists possess in adjusting costs through specific processing decisions. Such flexibility has four sources:

- Lack of national arrangement and description rules
- Lack of institutional policies
- Variability in processing component parts of specific groups of records
- The possibility of outside funding.

Unlike librarianship, where professionally established rules, such as those for cataloging, impose a minimum standard, archivists have no professionally sanctioned minimum processing standard. Without a minimum processing standard that all records in their care must meet, there is no professionally imposed baseline from which to estimate minimum processing costs. The latitude created by the lack of professionally established standards is reinforced by the lack of institutional standards. Most archives do not have institutional processing policies to guide the archivist. In many cases institutional practice creates a customary baseline for the archivist making processing decisions, but custom is often honored as much in the breach as in practice.

In part the lack of institutional processing standards reflects the archival propensity to determine processing needs on a case-by-case, section-by-section basis. Rather than employing a normative processing standard, many archivists base specific processing decisions upon predictive or intellectual criteria such as expected record use or comparative informational value. If the archivist anticipates a particular set of records will be heavily used or believes records have a peculiar intellectual value, intensive processing work may be undertaken. On the other hand, records the archivist considers of a more questionable character may be treated in a summary fashion. The decision-making process is further complicated by the practice of many archivists to differentiate between various component parts of the record set. Those parts of the record set that the archivist believes to have the greatest importance often receive additional attention and thus are arranged and described in more detail than other parts of the same set of records.[3]

Archivists also often have access to noninstitutional funding sources to underwrite processing costs. Public and private grant agencies that support cultural activity often will fund the processing of archival material. Archivists aware of grant funding possibilities may hope for such funding and sometimes anticipate receiving such funding when accepting specific records.

The four factors listed above create a very complex decision-making environment. Processing costs are not calculable by applying rigid formulas based on a fixed level of arrangement and description and comparing the resultant figure with the archives' budget. Rather, processing costs represent a range of possibilities that can readily be adjusted. Because of this ability to adjust costs to suit their needs, archivists often ignore processing costs in making selection decisions.

FIGURE 4-3.   Conservation/Preservation Costs Cluster

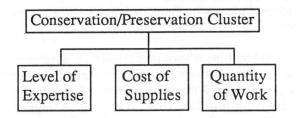

CONSERVATION

In discussing the preservation and conservation needs of records it is obvious that if physical preservation encompasses a sufficiently long period of time, most modern records will require major conservation effort. Modern paper is generally acidic and therefore unstable. Media such as photographs or magnetic pulses stored on a plastic base material have useful lives that are shorter than the worst paper. All recording media will eventually require conversion or stabilization. If this inevitable need were considered at the time of selection it would greatly increase the cost of accessioning specific records.

Currently, however, most archivists, when they consider selecting records for archival retention, do not consider the ultimate conservation costs, but rather look only at the records' immediate preservation and conservation needs. The attitude of most archivists continues to be that although the problem is real, the conservation needs of records that are in reasonably good shape today can be dealt with sometime in the indefinite future. Because of this attitude, the preservation/conservation cluster was defined as dealing with only the immediate needs of the records, rather than with long-term issues.

In this framework, the preservation/conservation component was originally configured in the same manner as the processing component. The same three elements, level of expertise, cost of supplies, and quantity of work were invoked and it was assumed that they would be defined and applied in a manner identical to that used for processing. The only qualification was that the cost of supplies element represented the marginal cost difference between normal office supplies and archival quality supplies; for example, the price difference between regular file folders and acid-free file folders.

Conservation/Preservation: Revisions

Not surprisingly, archivists approached conservation/preservation costs in the same way they approached processing costs. Great flexibility in making decisions again created a situation where archivists could adjust conservation/preservation costs. In contrast to processing, however, this flexibility was sometimes obtained by ignoring professionally sanctioned standards for preservation.

The archival community is aware that the physical existence of a document can be significantly prolonged by establishing and maintaining constant, rigid environmental controls in record storage and use areas.[4] Although these environmental standards are well-known, archivists sometimes ignore them. Even the best archival institutions, which have excellent environmental controls in place, often use environmentally substandard off-site storage facilities to house material when the total holdings of the archives exceed the storage capacity of the original facility.

Archivists often justify this action by claiming that it is better to place significant records in an archives, even if preservation conditions are less than ideal, than to expose the records to the vagaries of nonarchival control. Although there may be some truth in this justification, the willingness of archivists to accept new material and house it under preservation conditions that do not meet minimum standards reflects archivists willingness to ignore costs when they believe they are acting for a greater good. The specific character of that "greater good" is determined by professional principles and ethics. Changing the principles would change how archivists approach costs. Acting in the belief, for example, that it is professionally irresponsible to house records under conditions that do not meet minimum preservation standards, archivists would stop accepting new material when it could not be properly maintained. Preservation costs would thus be intimately linked to selection. Today, such an announcement would be almost unprecedented. Archivists considering costs not only exercise an extensive range of professional options, but often ignore costs associated with professionally recognized standards, basing their actions on a higher justification.

FIGURE 4-4. Storage Costs Cluster

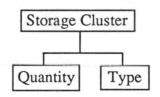

STORAGE

Storage, the fourth cluster in the costs module, was made up of two elements, the quantity of records and the type of storage required. The first element, quantity, reflects the fact that an archivist must find a place to put new acquisitions. The *type of storage* element recognizes that different record formats sometimes require unique storage space. Oversize items such as maps or blueprints often require special shelving. Photographs often require special care due to their chemical composition.

Storage: Revisions

Of all the costs associated with selection, archivists took storage most seriously. There are several explanations for this. Storage decisions cannot be postponed or avoided. An archivist may choose to do no processing on an accession and accept abominable preservation conditions, but storage space will have to be found for a new accession. Because of this, archivists have less flexibility in this area than in processing or preservation.

Still, there is a wide range of options available to cope with space issues. Examples of how extra storage space can be "found" are numerous. Extra space can be obtained by placing records in locations in the archives never designed for record storage. Vacant space not assigned to the archives but to which the archivist has access is sometimes "appropriated" and held under the assumption that possession is nine-tenths of the law. Records are sometimes stored in violation of fire codes, and cited archival fire hazards have sometimes taken years to rectify. These and other actions can be taken to "find" space. Furthermore, a specific archival accession is usually not so large that in and of itself it creates a space crisis. The problem is cumulative and thus frequently ignored when specific records are being considered for inclusion in the archives.

Despite this substantial flexibility, archivists selecting records concern themselves with space more than they do with any other financial issue. Beyond the obvious problem of finding a place to put the material, archivists have two additional reasons for taking space considerations seriously. First, in institutional budgetary competition, the need for additional space is an easy concept to present to senior administrators. Many administrators find arguments for authority control in description arcane, and perceive preservation-based demands to run air conditioning systems twenty-four hours a day as a waste of energy, but one need not be an archivist to understand that 10,000 feet of records cannot be housed in 5,000 feet of storage space. In such a situation something has to give, and with luck the administrator will give the archives more space.

In addition, the size of an archival institution's holdings has long been viewed by archivists as a crude indicator of the institution's importance. All other things being equal, to be the archivist of an archives with 20,000 linear feet of material is more prestigious than to administer an archives with 5,000 feet of holdings. Thus, because of the practical realities that space needs create for archivists, the usefulness of space in resource allocation discussions, and the "bragging rights" associated with the size of holdings, archivists have traditionally paid close attention to space and occasionally factored space into their selection decisions.

FIGURE 4-5. Reference Costs Cluster

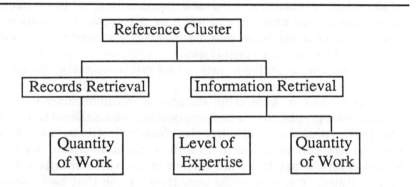

REFERENCE

The final cluster in the module was *reference*, comprised of two elements: *records retrieval* and *information retrieval*. The first element estimated the quantity of work needed to physically retrieve records for use by researchers. The second level evaluated the necessary level of expertise needed to provide intellectual access to the information in the records, as well as how frequently the reference staff of the archives would be called upon to supply intellectual access.

Reference: Revisions

In considering reference costs, the combination of archival flexibility and the difficulty in predicting future use created a situation where archivists had no way to estimate current costs. The ability to perform reference service is, in the first place, directly tied to the level of processing particular records receive. The more intensive the processing, the more complete and thorough reference service can be. Second, the level of reference service given by an individual archives is not subject to a professional standard. Rather, like processing, it is a matter of institutional policy and often really is defined by the conscience of the archivist. The level of reference assistance a researcher can expect can vary dramatically from archives to archives.

Third, estimating reference costs was complicated because the archivist was required to predict researcher use. Acquisition, processing, preservation/conservation, and storage costs may all have in them great amounts of flexibility, but ultimately each cost is under the archivist's control and can be established for a particular set of records. Future use is beyond the archivist's control and rests upon scholarly and nonscholarly factors. Scholarly factors such as future research trends and future published citations can significantly alter use patterns. Nonarchival factors such as the availability of travel grants, the ease with which researchers can reach the archives, or the surrounding area's appeal for tourism may all also affect use. An easily reached archives near a ski lodge may be frequently visited before and after weekends in which the snow is good.

Beyond the difficulty of estimating reference costs, philosophical issues exist over whether reference should be considered when records are accessioned. If, as is often stated, use is the ultimate justification for archival records, then a heavily used record set should be considered the most valuable of all archival material. Heavy use, however, increases reference cost and thus is a negative factor. As one wag summed up the apparent interaction of the value-of-information and cost modules, "a perfect collection, then, is one that has tremendous informational value, arrives at the archives in superb order, has no obvious conservation needs, requires only a little storage space, and is never used." Supporting use through reference service, some archivists asserted, was an obligatory, fixed expense that an archives accepts as part of its basic mission.

Although it is difficult to argue with the obligatory nature of supplying reference service for records in archival care, it is important to note the lack of a professional code defining the character and scope of that obligatory service. Without such a code the obligations of the archivist to researchers are undefined and the concept lacks true archival consequences. "Good" reference service is a laudable ambition rather than a true obligation. Furthermore, should such a standard be created in the future, new accessions would have to be measured against the possibility that the anticipated increase in use might cause the archives' reference service to drop below the minimum acceptable standard. The impact of accessioning a heavily used genealogical collection into an archives with an already understaffed reference service, for example, might push the general level of reference service below the archives' accepted professional standard. Reference costs exist, and the effect of professional standards for reference would be to heighten the importance of costs in selection.

TABLE 4-1. Rank Order of Costs-of-Retention Clusters

Cluster	Score
1. Storage	1.92
2. Processing	1.49
3. Conservation	1.39
4. Purchase/Transfer	1.36
5. Reference	1.19

THEORY VS. PRACTICE

Using the same one-to-four scale employed to evaluate the importance of elements and clusters in the *value of information* module, it is obvious that archivists do not consider costs a very important component in evaluating records. Conversations with archivists lead to the same conclusion: unless costs are extraordinary, they are not included in a selection decision.

If practicing archivists do not consider costs in selection, then the theoretical advice of G. Philip Bauer and others regarding the necessity of including costs in archival selection must be reconsidered. Given the divergence of theory and practice, which should take precedence? An answer to this question rests on three interrelated issues: the continuing flexibility of costs, the observance of standards, and the basic rationale justifying archival actions.

Part of the conflict between theory and practice arises in practitioners' broad ability to reconfigure costs to suit their immediate needs. It is extraordinarily difficult to create a theoretical framework that includes costs when practicing archivists can lower the financial implications attached to new accessions to virtually nothing beyond the cost of storage. Even if such a framework were created, there is today no compelling societal or professional reason for archivists to link costs to selection decisions.

The promulgation of professional standards for processing, preservation, or reference could create a baseline for estimating minimum selection costs. While an upper limit for costs would still be an institutional or personal archival decision, standards would create a minimum level of costs. Professional standards, however, are difficult to agree upon and even more difficult to enforce. Minimum preservation standards for various record formats are well-known among archivists, yet are frequently ignored in practice. Similarly, archival ethicists have long held that it is unacceptable for an archives to accept records knowing that it may be years or even decades before the material has been processed and is available for research, yet archivists continue to accept records under these conditions. Professional standards are meaningless if archivists fail to adhere to them.

The failure of archivists to implement standards that would introduce costs into the selection decision results from the previously discussed belief that it is better for records to be in an archives, whatever the status of the archives. Archival possession of historical material is accepted as the principal professional goal by many archivists and thus other goals are seen as secondary and dispensable in comparison to it. A professional ethic dominated by such a theoretical position makes it possible for archivists to ignore costs, or anything else, that would prevent records perceived as valuable from entering the archives. It is fair to ask whether or not the archival belief that an archivist's first obligation is to obtain records is justifiable. Is it better to house records in an archives, regardless of storage limitations, processing, preservation, and use, than to allow those records to remain outside the archival sphere?

As already noted, supporters of this position are likely to note that records outside the archives are exposed to great risk. The records' nonprofessional guardians frequently lack a sophisticated understanding of their importance, leading to a variety of foolish actions. Many archivists can tell stories in which the ultimate fate of significant documents was decided by whimsy or luck rather than by a sensitive appreciation of their importance and logical evaluation. Similarly, whimsy and luck have protected trivial records from elimination despite logical arguments for their destruction. To make a case for the importance of costs in archival selection, theoreticians must demonstrate a compelling reason for abandoning the idea that records are always better off in archives, and suggest an alternative to this idea.

The most compelling reason for changing the existing ethical order held by archivists is that it distorts the meaning of the word *archives* and creates among the public a false sense of what *archival care* entails. Archivists trade on the public's perception that an archives is a safe place for records. Archivists strive to educate the public that in an archives, records will be carefully preserved, adequately processed, and readily available for use. Archivists frequently complain about the application of the word *archives* to a wide variety of institutions and activities that, from their viewpoint, are distinctly nonarchival and do not provide the protection archivists associate with an archives. The public's confusion, however, is as much the fault of archivists as it is of the public's lack of education about archives. As a profession, archivists have not systematically defined what an archives is. Without professionally endorsed and implemented standards in areas such as preservation, processing, and reference—standards that define the character of an archives—anything can be called "the archives." Many professionally run archives adopt practices that are not so different from those of nonprofessionally run "archives." An educated public may rightly ask where the difference lies. Both groups profess to care "properly" for significant records, but the lack of objective criteria makes it impossible to validate either group's claim.

The desire among archivists to achieve professional recognition is a strong reason to urge the creation of professional standards for archives. If professionally endorsed standards existed for core archival activities such as reference services, preservation activities, and descriptive standards, it would be relatively simple to separate professionally run archives from their cut-rate imitators. The observance of professional standards would divide true archives from institutions using the name but not making the grade.

Establishing such standards and incorporating them into all aspects of archival work would, however, require a radical shift in the current approach of archivists towards record selection. Today it is acceptable for a professional archivist to accept new records regardless of their impact upon the program or the archives' ability to properly care for the records and make them available for use. If, however, the archival community defines a series of minimum standards for what constitutes an archives, for a particular institution to retain professional status professional standards would have to be applied to new accessions. The archives will have to have sufficient resources in place to properly deal with new records. If those resources do not exist the archivist will have to find additional resources, refuse to accept new records, or give up the institution's professional status. Accepting records that exceeded the capacity of the institution to meet professional standards would mean that the archivist was administering something other than an archives.

If professional standards were commonplace they would create an associated minimum cost standard against which to measure the impact of new accessions. The costs associated with processing, preserving, and referencing new records in a manner consistent with standards would form the inflexible baseline needed to include costs as a fixed component in selection decisions. Professionalization, then, becomes the ultimate rationale justifying the inclusion of costs in archival selection.

COSTS-OF-RETENTION: CONCLUSION

Today, archivists usually do not take costs into account when they evaluate records for selection. Traditionally, they have been able to ignore costs because of a combination of extreme financial flexibility, the lack of professional standards, and the belief that placing material in archival care is the most important action an archivist can take to preserve records. A changing archival worldview, however, reflecting the desire of many archivists to establish a recognized professional status, is driving the profession towards standards on a variety of fronts. The establishment of professional standards in areas such as arrangement, description, or preservation would create a minimum cost for accessioning new records that must be met by professional archives, and thus would create a reasonable baseline for establishing the cost of accepting specific records into the archives.

IMPLICATIONS-OF-THE-SELECTION DECISION

Each selection recommendation an archivist makes has implications for the archival repository. Some involve the policies and procedures of the archives itself. Most often, if a selection recommendation is implemented it will reinforce previous practices and policies. Some selection recommendations will be one time deviations from previous practices or policies that reflect unusual circumstances surrounding a particular selection recommendation. A few recommendations will establish new selection precedents or policies that redefine repository actions. The archival institution's relations with the outside world can also be affected by some selection recommendations. Administrators to whom the archivist is subordinate or a variety of third parties who are interested in the archives, including other institutional administrators, donors, and researchers, may be concerned about specific selection recommendations.

The implications of a selection recommendation may be positive, negative, or a little of both. A particular recommendation may establish beneficial new selection policies and win important friends for the archives, or a recommendation may obliterate years of carefully nurtured tradition and create implacable enemies. Most often, the implications of a particular recommendation will be minimal, neither changing policies nor being of particular interest to those outside the archives. This section explores how archivists view such recommendations in their work.

It is important to preface this discussion, however, with an acknowledgment of the subjective and controversial nature of the *implications* module. Recommendations about the implications of a selection are the most subjective judgments archivists make. Judgments about the wishes, actions, and reactions of nonarchival actors to a selection recommendation are difficult. Such judgments require the skill of a keen psychological observer and the ability to accurately predict future events, neither of which is a professional skill taught in archival training. The idea of interjecting costs into selection recommendation has been discussed for almost a half-century, but it remains a controversial idea. The idea of consciously considering the implications of the selection decision has existed in the archival literature for less than a decade, and is more controversial than costs.[5]

The initial justification for the implications module was the observation that many archivists link selection recommendations with a variety of other archival and nonarchival factors. Some archivists thought as much about who the records came from and what the implications of the contribution might be for their institution as they did about the actual information in the records. Whatever the records' character, an unsolicited contribution to a university archives by the institution's president was rarely determined to be inappropriate by the archivist. Similarly, records that were of interest to past or potential financial benefactors usually were examined by the archivist with a somewhat different eye than records not having the support of an important patron. Nonarchival factors affected selection.

Although the existence of the implications module in selection can be empirically demonstrated, the ethical legitimacy of it has been called into question by some archivists. If an archivist begins with a premise similar to that of Herman Kahn, that archives exist principally for cultural reasons, then it is possible to argue that noncultural factors should not be allowed to influence the documentation maintained. Just as an institution's cultural heritage should not be the result of this year's budget, so too the cultural mission of an archives should not fall victim to contemporary foibles and politics. Later in this section the theoretical legitimacy of including implications in the selection recommendation will be discussed.

EXTERNAL RELATIONS

As originally conceived, the *external relations* component was divided into two parts: *source* and *other parties*. *Source* was defined as that individual or corporate entity from which the records came. *Other parties* were any other individuals or corporate entities that might be interested in the outcome of the selection recommendation. In a university setting, for example, the president's office might be concerned about records donated by an influential alumni. Archives user communities, such as historians or genealogists, are also *other parties* who might be interested in the outcome of a particular selection recommendation. Additional *other parties* might be people named in the records under consideration, for example, the personally identified subjects in the research files of a sociologist.

FIGURE 4-6.   External Relations Cluster—Original Configuration

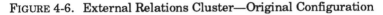

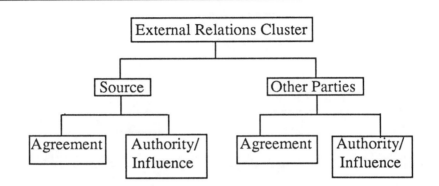

In considering either source or other party relations, it was originally assumed that the archivist would consider two elements: *agreement* and *authority/influence*. It was assumed that the greater the degree of agreement between the selection recommendation and the wishes of those not directly working in the library, the better the situation. *Agreement*, it was thought, promoted harmonious relations. The second element considered was the *authority* or *influence* of the external parties. Although harmony through agreement was to be sought, both the advantages to the archives created by harmony and the disadvantages created by a lack of harmony largely depended upon the clout of the external parties. Harmony with weak, ineffective administrators might be pleasant but not particularly beneficial, whereas disharmony with a well-organized user group, such as a local genealogical society, might create a crisis.

Although the basic ideas used in constructing the external relations cluster appeared to be confirmed by participating archivists, the clusters were incorrectly organized. Rather than systematically considering the likely reaction of various groups who might be interested in the selection recommendation, archivists tended to approach the problem in a more linear, directed fashion. Archivists first looked for groups with significant authority or influence who might be concerned about a specific selection recommendation. If the archivist decided that such a group or groups existed, then the archivist thought about how they would react to the selection recommendation. Retrospective reading of management literature suggested that this kind of decision-making structure is relatively common in organizations and that the original design of the cluster was improperly conceptualized. The conceptual flaw can most easily be explained by the principal investigator's lack of administrative experience.[6]

FIGURE 4-7. External Relations Cluster—Original Configuration

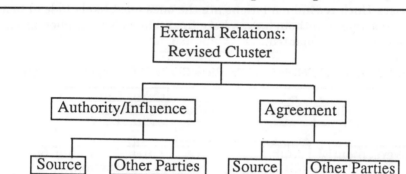

Although this reconfigured external relations cluster is an improvement over the original structure, it probably is still incomplete or in some way inadequate. Archivists have written very little about the effects of the external environment on repository management and activities. As open systems, archives, like libraries, receive from, contribute to, and interact with the organizations that surround them.[7] Traditionally, however, archivists have been preoccupied with internal functions and activities; with issues such as how to appraise items in a collection or how to arrange and describe their holdings. Archivists have not systematically considered the repository's external roles or thought about archives as part of an open system. This lack of analysis creates significant lacunae, because understanding selection is to some extent contingent upon understanding the exchange and interaction between archives and individuals outside of the repository. In part, a better understanding of the selection recommendation depends upon future work investigating the general nature of archival repositories as open systems.

Internal Policies and Practices

The internal policies and practices cluster represents a review by the archivist to determine if recommendations about various selection criteria and costs are justifiable. Most often the review is performed very rapidly by the archivist saying to him or herself that when the records at hand were considered, the archives' official policies and informal customs were followed. Sometimes the archivist will need to justify a "one time" variation in a policy or a custom. This justification may be done through a written document, but most often it will be a matter of the archivist reaching a personal conclusion that the variation is justified. On rare occasions a recommendation may alter the policies or customs of the institution. These occasions create the greatest amount of thought, and often will be preceded by consultation with other archivists. Such recommendations are the ones most likely to lead to a written document, although even here the archivist's recommendation may remain undocumented.

FIGURE 4-8.   Internal Policies and Practices Cluster—Original Configuration

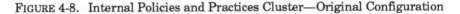

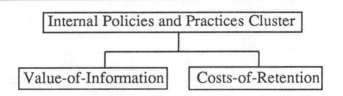

Internal Policies and Practices: Reinterpretation

Although archivists participating in the study found no fundamental flaw in this cluster, neither did they find any particular merit to it. In general the cluster received very few favorable or unfavorable comments. In reconsidering the cluster in the light of management literature, it would appear that a more fruitful, and probably more accurate, interpretation would group these considerations according to managerial concerns such as personnel, facilities and equipment, output, materials, organizational structure and communication, and finances, rather than illuminating the concerns solely by the exclusive and peculiar light of selection.[8]

Because the elements in this module were not well conceived, it is difficult to draw many far-reaching conclusions from the rank order in which archivists placed them. Two general conclusions, therefore, are all that can safely be offered. First, the concerns of archival administrators regarding external factors tended to be similar to those of other administrators in open systems. This suggests that much of the library literature on management would be applicable to the archival setting. Second, despite theoretical objections similar to those raised about costs, in practice archivists demonstrated a reasonable amount of concern over the implications of a selection recommendation.

TABLE 4-2. Rank Order of Internal Policies and Practices Elements

Element	Average Score
1. Authority concerns	2.33
2. Source concerns	2.17
3. Third party concerns	2.12
4. Internal Policy - V of I	2.08
5. Agreement Concerns	1.96
6. Internal Policy - Costs	1.92

The fact that most archivists in the test group did consider the implications of a selection recommendation before reaching their ultimate decision seems to confirm the theoretical question of legitimacy. To answer the question, it is useful to place selection recommendations into a broad, institutional policy context.

Those who argue that selection is primarily a cultural action implicitly suggest that selection is the most important action an archives takes. Selection policy, therefore, becomes the primary institutional policy, with all other institutional goals and desires becoming secondary to finding and retaining appropriate cultural documentation. Looking at selection policy as one part of a system of institutional policies, however, recasts this view. An archival institution will have a variety of goals and policies. If no automatic assumptions are made regarding the ranking of those policies, the archivist may choose to subordinate selection policy to other institutional policies or needs.

One example of the subordination of selection policy for a greater good is found in efforts of various archivists to raise funds for new archival buildings. In the process of courting those who control the financial wherewithal to fund construction, whether private donors or governmental administrators, archivists often use record accessioning as a tool to make friends. By accepting records considered important by potential donors or the individual who controls funding, regardless of the records' relationship to selection policy, the archivist seeks to influence them to supply the funding needed for a new building.

Archivists who define their institutions in exclusively cultural terms may find the practice of flattering those with funds through record accessions akin to making a pact with the devil for one's soul. Other archivists, however, will point out that when properly executed the result is not the loss of the archives' soul but rather the expansion and enrichment of its program through new physical facilities. One midwestern archivist, for example, accepted an estimated 500 linear feet of "junk" records from potential financial contributors, but as a result was able to fund the construction of a new archives building with approximately 20,000 linear feet of storage space. The net gain of 19,500 feet of state-of-the-art storage space allowed the archives to expand its program and house important records that could never have fit in its previous accommodations. In addition, subsequent reappraisal work slowly whittled away at the "junk" brought in during the fundraising activity.

When the archivist views selection as part of an overall set of institutional policies, considering the impact of a specific selection recommendation upon the entire range of policies is a logical administrative act. In many cases the implementation of the archives primary mission statement may involve more than simply collecting the right records. When this occurs, it seems logical that selection policy, like any other institutional policy, must bend in order to facilitate the institution's primary mission.

TABLE 4-3. Rank Order of Modules

Module	Average Value
1 Value-of-Information	2.52
2 Implications-of-the- Selection-Decision	2.09
3 Costs-of-Retention	1.47

CONCLUSIONS

Before concluding this section of the analysis, it is profitable to consider the relative ranking the survey participants assigned to the three modules. It is not surprising that the *value of information* module, long accepted by archivists as the heart of the appraisal process, was considered the most important. What is more interesting is the relative order of the remaining two modules and the relatively even spacing between each of them.

Archivists have long debated the theoretical relevance of costs and ignored the implications of the selection recommendation. It is interesting, however, that in practice archivists consider the implications of the selection recommendation far more important than the much-discussed cost factors. Implications matter to archivists, costs apparently do not.

What is also interesting is the relatively even spacing between the three modules. It is not the case that all are equal, or that archivists think first about the value of the information in records and then give equal attention to the other two modules. Rather, archivists first think about the information, then sometimes worry about the implications of the selection recommendation, then very occasionally consider costs. This ordering has significance in structuring future practical decision-making models for selection.

Endnotes

1. The market value of many records is determined by several factors besides their informational content. Artifactual concerns such as autographs or events occurring simultaneously with the creation of a document will frequently affect market price. Such concerns, however, are beyond the scope of this work.

2. In some cases the donor may be indirectly compensated for giving records to a repository by claiming a charitable deduction on his or her federal income tax. Current tax law, however, is designed to limit such deductions.

3. See Megan Floyd Desnoyers, "When is a Collection Processed," *Midwestern Archivist* 7 (1982):5-23.

4. See Mary Lynn Ritzenthaler, *Archives & Manuscripts: Conservation: A Manual on Physical Care and Management* (Chicago: Society of American Archivists, 1983).

5. Frank Boles and Julia Marks Young, "Exploring the Black Box: The Appraisal of University Administrative Records," *American Archivist* 48 (Spring 1985): 121-140. This is the first formal suggestion to include implications of the selection recommendation in the decision-making process, although the idea had existed for some time prior to this publication.

6. One of the earliest and most influential articles on this topic was Fremont E. Kast and James E. Rosenzweig, "General Systems Theory: Applications for Organizations and Management," *Academy of Management Journal* 15 (December 1972): 447-465. At the time the module was first conceptualized, neither Frank Boles nor Julia Young had held major administrative positions.

7. Maurice P. Marchant, "The Library as an Open System," in *Participative Management in Academic Libraries* (Westport, CT: Greenwood Press, 1976): 13-28; Howard E. Aldrich and Jeffrey Pfeffer, "Environments of Organizations," in Beverly P. Lynch, ed., *Management Strategies for Libraries: A Basic Reader* (New York: Neal-Schuman, 1985): 186-221; Beverly P. Lynch, "The Academic Library and Its Environment," *College and Research Libraries* 35 (March 1974): 126-32.

8. See G. Edward Evans, *Management Techniques for Librarians* 118-120.

5

Institutional Differences and the Usefulness of Quantification in Selection

Having considered the basic elements of selection, two other issues related to the selection decision remain to be discussed. One is the issue of numbers. The project methodology linked a quantification system to the selection process. Although some thought this a foolish linkage, other archivists had hoped that quantification would prove a useful tool for increasing the precision of selection decisions. In part, this project tested that thesis, as well as the broader thesis that selection decisions could be represented in a numerical fashion.

Differences in how various archives use record selection criteria is the second issue to be considered in this chapter. When archivists discuss selection decisions they often imply that a universally valid approach for making such decisions exists. Archivists seemingly assume that a single list of selection criteria can be applied more or less equally in all cases. Data gathered during this project cast serious doubt on this assumption, suggesting instead that institutional policy and mission strongly influence the importance of selection criteria.

QUANTIFICATION: INTRODUCTION

Quantification techniques were used in the study for two purposes. First, quantification served as a tool to investigate archival selection itself. Insights were obtained into how archivists view selection. A second, subsidiary reason for using quantification was to determine if a numerical scheme could be devised to assist archivists in selecting records. Quantification proved very helpful as an explanatory tool. As a practical, day-to-day decision-making tool, however, the quantification system employed was unworkable. To understand the methodology used, the mathematical system employed during the study will be described here, followed by a report on the practical effectiveness of the methodology. We conclude with some thoughts on the overall role of numerical approaches to selection.

System Explanation

The quantification system used in the project consisted of four discrete parts: *element scales, element weights, threshold values,* and *"kickers."* Each played a specific role in reaching a selection decision.

The element scales were the first part of the system. A zero to five scale was constructed for every element in each module. These values quantified the archivist's qualitative judgment regarding the presence or absence of an element in the records being evaluated. A score of five meant that the particular element was very well represented in the records at hand. A score of zero meant that the element was not present in the records under evaluation. The numbers in between zero and five represented a qualitative judgment somewhere between all or nothing. How this worked in practice was fairly simple. To cite an example, if records under evaluation had obvious continuing administrative use, the archivist rated the records a five on the scale. If the records clearly had no continuing administrative purpose, the archivist rated the documents a zero. If the archivist's evaluation led him or her to believe the administrative value was somewhere between all or nothing, the scale score fell somewhere between five and zero. To avoid endless hairsplitting, archivists were asked to use only whole numbers on the scale.

Using numbers in this way is not a new idea. In the early 1980s the Washington State Archives developed an appraisal matrix that linked numbers to the appraisal elements used by the archives. The rationale underlying both the Washington system and the ranking process used in this study was borrowed from public opinion survey techniques. Just as a numerical scale can be used to quantify the strength of public opinion about a politician or a social issue, it seemed that archivists should be able to use numerical scales to quantify qualitative judgments about the presence or absence of each selection element in records. Providing archivists can agree upon the elements of selection, and the question each element asks of the records, assigning a reasonably valid numerical score is straightforward.[1]

After having used scales to assign numerical values to qualitative assessments of records, archivists used the second part of the methodology, weights (multipliers), to adjust the numbers to reflect the element's importance to the archives. It was hypothesized that all selection elements were not of equal importance in all archives. To reflect this hypothesis, archivists were asked to examine the elements of selection independently from any specific record evaluation, and rank the elements by their importance in the archivist's own institution. A one to four scale was used for this ranking, with a score of four representing an element that was considered very important in selection and a score of one being an element that was almost never thought about when looking at records. For example, an institutional archives might place particular emphasis on records originating from the organization's senior officers. If an institution weighted the position in organization element equal to 4, and the records being examined were given an element scale score of 5, the element's weighted score would be 4 x 5, equalling 20.

This multiplication process was crude. Using the scale values directly as multipliers assumed that an element always considered was four times more important than an element rarely considered, without having any real reason for defining the mathematical relationship in this way. However, without any prior studies available from which to assign values, a crude multiplier was viewed as better than no multiplier at all. The approach also incorporated the assumption that since weights reflected institutional policies, once weights were established they remained the same for all record selections. Although this assumption, like the use of element scales, was not unprecedented, neither was it a widely accepted idea in the archival community.[2]

Evaluating the Records

The basic system of weighted scales was modified by thresholds and "kickers". The third part of the methodology, a threshold, determined the applicability of each element to a particular selection evaluation. It was hypothesized that if records possess an insignificant amount of a particular criteria, that is if the element was assigned a value below the threshold score on a particular scale, the element could be ignored. The threshold score was a single, whole number, from 0 to 5, established for each element scale. Once established the threshold value for an element remained unchanged. To illustrate a threshold, an institution might decide that unless the *position in hierarchy* element was significant (defined as receiving a score of 4 or more) it would be ignored. Thus if a record scored less than four on this element scale, the element, and the number associated with it, would drop out of all subsequent selection considerations and calculations.

The rationale underlying thresholds was a pragmatic one. Some archivists noted that when they evaluated records, they often concluded that although a particular selection element was present, it was too insignificant to merit consideration. The archivist simply ignored the element when evaluating the records. Thresholds incorporated this observation into the mathematical system.

The fourth and last parts of the system were "kickers." In specific archival settings, if a key element was present, such as a high position in the organization, or records documenting enduring legal functions, the records would be saved regardless of any other element. Kickers created a way to mathematically incorporate the idea that some records are automatically "kicked into the archives." The rationale underlying kickers was the observation of some archivists that sometimes they were able to make a selection decision based on the presence of a single, particularly important, record characteristic. To paraphrase a colleague: "If it's the president's papers, I don't have to think about it, I save them."

Practical Applications

The best way to summarize the concepts of scales, weights, thresholds, and kickers is to review quickly how participating archivists used them. Participants first looked at their institutional policies to determine the relative importance of each element; that is, they established weights and placed the numbers on a master "Appraisal Decision Form." Second, participants again looked at institutional policies to determine if thresholds and/or kickers should be established for any element. Having established weights, thresholds, and kickers, these values were incorporated into selection decisions about records. In the absence of any kickers, records were given a score on each element scale, and where threshold values existed, that score was compared against the threshold. If the element scale score was less than the threshold value, the element was considered insignificant and ignored. A scale score above the threshold value would rate the element as important enough to merit further consideration and it would be multiplied by its weight, if one had been established for that element, to calculate a weighted element score.

The calculations that tied together all of these elements into a final score were relatively complex. First, the sum of the weighted element scores for each module was computed. Then each of the weighted element values of the 19 elements in module one (see chapter 3) were totaled into a final module score, as were the 12 elements in module two and the six elements in module three.[3] As already noted, if a score failed to reach the element threshold it was omitted from the module summation. The three resulting numbers were used to construct a cost-benefit ratio. The score for module one, the value of information, was placed in the ratio's numerator. The score of module two, the costs of retention, was placed in the denominator. The score of module three, the policy implications, was added to either module one or module two, depending upon whether the policy implications were considered beneficial or detrimental to the archives. If the impact was beneficial, policy implications were added to the value of information; if the impact was detrimental, policy implications were added to the costs of retention. A final ratio was then calculated, representing the selection score.

The rationale for casting the final equation in the form of a cost-benefit ratio rested primarily upon the writings of Bauer and Cook. The decision reflected archival thinking that saw records as having certain values while incurring certain costs, and suggested that the best records would have the greatest value for the smallest cost. Although such a hypothesis was controversial, it was a logical way to broadly explain the relationship that exists between the various elements of selection.

QUANTIFICATION: DISAPPOINTING RESULTS

The ultimate test of this cumbersome mathematical mechanism was its efficacy in evaluating records. Archivists who struggled with the intricacies of the system were disappointed with the result. In short, they found the system did not work as a practical selection tool. Neither the final ratio nor the module scores accurately predicted absolute or relative record value. As a research tool to help explain selection, however, quantification was very successful.

At the broadest possible level, that the ratio scores did not result in a number that had an absolute predictive value and permitted comparisons of collections across institutions was not surprising, or even particularly troubling. Three reasons explain interinstitutional differences. Institutions differed in how they assigned element scale scores. Archivists in some "shops" were "easy" graders, others "hard." Different patterns of element exclusion created by the number of elements assigned thresholds and the value assigned to particular thresholds also affected the final result. An archivist who rigorously pared the overall number of elements by frequently assigning high threshold values generated lower final scores than an archivist who used everything. Most important, differences in institutional weights affected the final score. Some archivists assigned more large weights than other archivists, and some institutional policy frameworks led to the assigning of a larger number of weights than in other institutions. All these practices resulted in institutions ending up with final ratios that made no sense when compared to one another.

What was disappointing was that the final ratio score also proved inconsistent within individual institutions. For a mathematical system to be a practical selection tool, at the minimum it should generate results that consistently rank an institution's records. Ideally, the records the archivist thought had the "best" information should receive the highest information module score, with the remaining records falling into a numerical order of descending value. Similarly, the final ratio should have established a ranked order of records, although not necessarily the same order as that obtained from the information module, since collections with high costs would rank lower on this listing. Unfortunately, the scores collections received did not consistently rank the collections in the order the institution's archivists would have placed them in using their normal evaluative techniques.

The nature of the problem can be exemplified by results generated at the Center for Archival Studies, Bowling Green State University (BGSU). BGSU was a particularly interesting test site because the archives have extremely diverse holdings. Archivists there applied the mathematical system to the evaluation of college and university records, traditional manuscript collections, and public records. BGSU's archivists evaluated eight record groups at the record group level, and one record group at the series level, resulting in a total of 11 evaluations. Three evaluations were of public records, three were of university administrative records, and the remaining five were of manuscript material. The final results are shown in Table 5-1.

TABLE 5-1. Record Evaluation Scores, Bowling Green State University[4]

Collection	Ratio	Calc.	Record Type
1 Bloom Township Road	41.2/1	216+31/6	Public Records
2 BGSU Personnel Files	38.8/1	195+38/6	University
3 Bloom Township School	38.6/1	201+31/6	Public Fund Accounts
4 BGSU History Dept.	35.5/1	116+26/4	University Chair's Corres.
5 Pauli Papers Printed	31.0/1	184+2/6	Manuscript Material
6 Bloom Township	29.3/1	145+31/6	Public Chattel Mortgages
7 Hill/Morgan Papers	28.7/1	170+2/6	Manuscript
8 Pauli Papers	19.7/1	195+2/10	Manuscript Literary Documents
9 Toledo Symphony	19/6/1	178+18/10	Manuscript
10 Pauli Papers	18.1/1	179+2/10	Manuscript Correspondence
11 BGSU Treasurer's	10.8/1	148+24/16	University Subject File

The rank order of collections as established by the final ratio varied significantly from the order of importance BGSU's archivists placed upon the collections. The Toledo Symphony records, for example, ranked ninth in terms of the ratio score, yet the archivists who worked with this material considered it the most valuable collection of the 11 evaluated. The three Township record groups were considered by the archivists of middle value or less, yet two Township record groups scored first and third in the ratio ranking. Part of the reason for this result was the fact that the archivists at BGSU, like other test participants, generally did not factor costs into their normal evaluative procedures. Because the Toledo Symphony's records had somewhat higher costs due to conservation problems, it received a lower ratio score, while at the same time the Township records, because they were well organized and in relatively good physical shape, had relatively low costs.

Costs, however, do not adequately explain why the Symphony's records were so poorly ranked or why the Township records ranked so highly. If costs were excluded, and the collections were ranked solely on the information module score, the Toledo Symphony's records still finished a poor seventh, while the positions of the Township records actually improved from the first and third to the first and second positions.[5] Nor did the inclusion of module three, the implications module, help solve the difference between the archivists' judgment and the numbers. Including the implications module in the evaluation ranking raised the Symphony's papers to the fifth position, and returned the Township records to their original rank order positions of first and third. This result still under-represented the value archivists placed on the Symphony collection while, in the archivists' view, overvaluing the township records.[6] A similar disparity between the ranking of collections evaluated through the test methodology and the judgment of participating archivists was observed at all of the test sites.

Discussing the Selection Criteria

If quantification did not prove a useful predictive tool, it did prove a valuable technique for furthering the discussion among archivists of specific selection decisions, thus improving the project's understanding of the selection process. What was discovered was that in both abstract discussions of selection and specific applications of elements to records, archivists could come to verbal agreement that an element of selection was important, without really agreeing on anything. Words like *important, substantive*, or *significant*, held different meanings for different archivists. In one particularly striking instance, a test site that believed its archivists had a general consensus about selection standards found that when the staff was forced to assign numbers to those standards there was great divergence. The use of a numerical methodology was responsible for obtaining this kind of insight.

Analyzing the Results

The obvious conclusion drawn from these results was that the mathematical methodology used here was not sufficiently accurate to use as a practical selection tool, but that it did serve a valuable purpose in furthering qualitative discussion of records. Having reached these conclusions, two broad analytical questions remain. First, could changes be made in the methodology proposed here to make it a better predictive instrument? Could a revised version, for example, be used as the beginnings of an expert system for selection? Whatever possibilities exist for reinvigorating the mathematical system used here, a second question regarding the overall usefulness of a numerical methodology in selection evaluation needs to be considered. In the abstract, can numbers be useful selection aids, or is selection an unquantifiable art?

Improving the predictive ability of the methodology used in this test, or developing a new methodology to supersede this one, would be a challenging task. Before the predictive ability of the mathematical system could be improved, it would likely be necessary to first improve archivists' basic understanding of selection. The methodology used in the experiment was based upon a taxonomy that incorporated archivists' present understanding of selection. A taxonomy, although it orders and classifies the elements in a system, does not explain the relationships between the system's elements. The methodology used here made the assumption that the relationships between the various elements in selection could be expressed through simple additive procedures, augmented where necessary by multiplication. It further assumed that the overall relationship could be adequately represented through a cost-benefit ratio. The results of the experiment suggest that the relationships between the elements of selection are not this simple. Adding up the various weighted elements scores, dividing information value by costs, then including a "fudge" factor of implications is too simplistic a representation to explain the evaluative process that underlies selection.

To develop a mathematical predictive system the relationship between the elements of selection and the way in which they interact would have to be better explained. Assuming the taxonomy itself is correct, it would first still be necessary to define independent and dependent elements. It seems to be the case that some selection elements depend upon others for their importance. For example, an inter-relationship often exists between the position in an institutional hierarchy of a record's creator, and the continuing administrative value of the records. Senior officers tend to create records with longer administrative use. This and similar relationships need to be carefully defined.

Second, relationships between particular groups of elements may exist which makes their cumulative importance greater than their individual weighted or unweighted scores. For example, a senior administrative official, authoring a policy document discussing a subject deemed of national importance, and for which his or her institution was considered a pioneer, might create a record widely acknowledged to be of great significance. The value of that record might exceed the value of the sum of the selection elements because such documentation serves as the qualitative archetype that scholars use to unravel the past. A better understanding of the cumulative impact of elements is needed.

Third, it would be necessary to incorporate a dynamic capability into the system. As presented here, the mathematical methodology was static. Information, costs, and implications were fixed values. In the real world, however, these are dynamic, fluid concepts. Information can be enhanced by expending additional funds to refine organizational defects or create improved descriptive tools. Costs can be modified or negated by lowering descriptive standards or by finding funding sources that are outside of normal budgetary channels, such as grants. Implications can change based on assiduous education campaigns or the normal changes that time brings to all institutions and offices. Although the issues of independent and dependent elements, critical clusters of elements, and internal dynamism, can be expressed succinctly, creating answers would be a time-consuming process.[7]

Developing Fuzzy-Logic Systems

The potential complexity of the analytical problem can be understood by comparing it to efforts to develop a computerized expert system for chemistry. Computerized expert systems use "fuzzy logic" to solve problems, as humans do. Fuzzy logic systems are based upon defined, wide-ranging, yet detailed rules that represent the thought processes used by a recognized human expert to arrange, analyze, and solve a discipline related problem. The difficulty in copying a human expert's analytical skills is that humans use very large sets of rules which interrelate in subtle ways to solve problems. One study, for example, estimated that a Noble Laureate in chemistry has at his or her disposal somewhere between 50,000 to 100,000 rules used to arrange and analyze information.[8] Although an adequate expert system for chemistry, or selection, could use an abridged set of rules, the challenge of understanding even one percent of a true expert's decisionmaking paths, 500 to 1,000 rules, would be formidable.

A workable mathematical methodology that accurately reflects all the components of archival thought on selection, and organizes that thought into an accurate reflection of an archivist's judgment, does not appear to be an easily obtained goal. It may, in fact, be unobtainable, but to conclude this based on the preliminary and simplistic work of this study would be premature. Even if the goals of an accurate predictive mathematical methodology or an expert system proved, in the long run, to be unobtainable, continuing research in this area is important for the qualitative insights it would yield into the selection process. The effort to establish underlying relationships between elements in the selection taxonomy, to create an overall explanation that describes how archivists select records, and to define the rules archivists use to make decisions, are all important qualitative issues that can be pursued as part of the development of a mathematical selection methodology. As an area of pure research, work on a mathematical selection methodology could yield important insights into the nature of selection itself.

Usefulness of Numerical Methodology

If the archival community is not likely to soon have a practical, predictive mathematical methodology to aid in record evaluation, is there any purpose that numbers can serve in selection? This is the second major question posed by the quantification issue and the answer to it is more positive than the answer to the first. As has already been noted, this study suggests that a numerical methodology is a useful device for forwarding the discussion of selection decisions. This ability to improve archivist's discussions about selection evaluations is important and useful. It exists independent of any predictive power the numbers possess.

The usefulness of numbers to forward discussions regarding decisions has been implicitly recognized in several current archival projects and in a number of nonarchival fields, such as preservation microphotography, museum selection, and library science. One example of a mathematical selection aid used by archivists, which has already been referred to, is a matrix developed by the Washington State Archives. Fifteen record characteristics were considered in the matrix, each receiving a score from five to zero, depending upon the qualities the records displayed. *Age / Scarcity*, for example, was the first characteristic listed. Five points were assigned to pre-1900 records, four points for records dating from 1900 to 1920, three points for records from 1921 to 1940, two points for records from 1941 to 1960, and post-1961 records received either one point or zero points, depending upon whether the records were considered generally available or widely available. A similar point scale was developed for each characteristic.[9]

While the Washington State Archives matrix represents the most sophisticated day-to-day use of a numerical methodology among archivists, several other major projects have used qualitative methodologies that could have been easily quantified. The two most prominent examples are studies undertaken regarding the records of the Massachusetts Superior Court and the Federal Bureau of Investigation (FBI). In both projects, records' characteristics were classified on a *high, medium, low,* or *no* continuum for one or more elements. This continuum could have been easily represented by a zero to four scale.[10]

In the preservation community the Alabama Newspaper project exemplifies the use of a numerical methodology to assist in making decisions. The project developed a numerical form to determine if a particular newspaper should be microfilmed. After articulating five exclusion criteria that would automatically disqualify a paper for microfilming, a 20-element criteria list was drawn up to determine if a paper should be filmed. The form's scales were designed so that the newspaper either displayed or lacked the criteria. If the criteria were present ten points were allotted. Weighting was also employed; in that two elements, deemed particularly significant, were assigned a value of 20, rather than ten, points.[11]

The museum community has also been interested in quantification schemes. For example, the Children's Museum of Indianapolis has created a numerical ranking system for its textile collection. Several major questions, including child and adult interest potential, function, representativeness, amount of documentation, and association with an important person, place, or event are ranked on a one to five scale, with the points being added together to reach a final score.[12]

The library community also uses numerical methodologies to assist in decisionmaking. Among many efforts has been work to devise a numerical system to assist librarians in collection development. John Rutledge and Luke Swindler, for example, have devised a complex system involving six selection criteria: subject, intellectual content, potential use, relation to collection, bibliographic considerations, and language. These criteria were ranked on a weighted numerical scale that was heavily skewed in favor of subject, content, and use. Subject could receive a maximum score of 30 points, intellectual content a maximum score of 25, potential use a maximum of 20, relation to collection, bibliographic considerations, and language a maximum score of 12, 8, and 5 points respectively.[13]

Although some of these applications are controversial and their predictive ability suffers from the same problems that limited the mathematical methodology used in this study, this short list of applications makes it clear that the use of numbers has a strong appeal. Numbers can establish a regular method for making judgments, a rational vehicle for noting and discussing disagreements in judgment, and a consistent way of reporting decisions. The ability to standardize, discuss, and report on decisions is important to any organization. Archivists share this need and thus, like many other professionals, are attempting to develop tools that meet it.[14]

If numerical methodology is useful for rationalizing, systematizing, and communicating functions, then it is legitimate to ask if the mathematical methodology used in this project displayed these characteristics. As has already been reported, many test participants found it was

useful in these areas. However, they and the minority of test participants who did not find the methodology useful even for this application
noted problems that should be addressed to improve the methodology's
power in these areas. Specific problems included the construction of
quantitative scales that accurately captured the qualitative nuances of
the various elements, the need to incorporate negative perceptions into
scales, a better understanding and mathematical representation of
weights, and a too-narrow application of both thresholds and kickers.

Constructing Element Scales

Constructing scales that accurately reflect archivists' qualitative
judgments proved difficult. Even when archivists agree on the qualitative characteristics of an element it can be difficult, but the problem was
exacerbated by disagreements among archivists over qualitative issues.
A typical disagreement occurred, for example, in discussing the most
desirable outcome for the eleventh element in the *value of information*
module, the intellectual content of a set of records when compared to
the repository's holdings. The initial element scale ran from redundant
(zero) to unique (five). However, some archivists argued that the most
desirable outcome for this element was not that the records proved
unique but rather that they complement and supplement existing
records. In this framework, supplementary/complementary records, not
unique records, were considered of greatest value and thus should be
given the highest scale score. Although element scales in all the modules
suffered from qualitative disagreements, and from the general difficulty
experienced in accurately reflecting qualitative concerns numerically,
the elements within the *implications* module proved particularly trou-
blesome in both regards.

Constructing scales that more accurately reflect what archivists
look for when they evaluate records would be an important step in
improving the systematizing and communicative power of the methodology. In an ultimate sense there is no final construct, since archivists'
understanding of selection elements will always be evolving. However,
continuing work by archivists to better understand exactly what the
elements of selection are, and the specific factor archivists are focusing
on when they say that records possess an element, would lead to ever
more accurate definitions and a better set of scales. These, in turn, would
make the numbers derived from element scales more useful in communicating selection evaluations.

A second problem that some archivists perceived in the system used
here was the inability of scales to incorporate negative perceptions. As
presented, the scales began with zero, meaning the element had no
importance or was absent, and increased to five as the element's import-

ance increased. In some cases, however, elements could have strongly negative influences which could not be reflected in the study's scale value system. For example, when policy issues were being considered, the decision to retain certain records might have strongly positive effects or strongly negative effects. In discussing the scale value for agreement of third-party sources, one institution pointed out that among conflicting groups of third parties, accepting one group's papers could alienate the other group. A zero score on the appropriate element scale did not adequately reflect the negative effects of the situation on the repository. Similarly, in considering costs certain decisions represent cost benefits. Accepting papers might mean the ability to attract temporary grant funding or establish new permanent staff positions. Negative scales would also have created an elegant way to deal with the generally negative impact of the illegibility, understandability, and use limitation elements. A scale that ran from negative five to positive five would better represent the actual possibilities that exist in the real world.

Weighting the Value Elements

Weights presented a problem because of the arbitrary way their mathematical value was assigned. As already noted, in constructing the system, weights were limited to values ranging from one to four. This decision was made so that weight values could be quickly assigned based on the relative importance of elements in an institution, but the method was not broad enough to allow the weights to truly reflect the importance institutions placed on the elements. For example, the policy framework in an archival institution might dictate that the *position in hierarchy* element was the most important single element. Archivists in the institution might agree that it was of more importance than the combined effect of several other elements, such as timespan, credibility, scarcity, potential use, and use limitations. Since *position in hierarchy* was more significant than the other five elements, its maximum weighted scale value should be larger than the combined weighted scale values of the other five elements, but in the mathematical system used this was not possible.

Another problem with weights was in the assumption that one set of weights could describe the overall policies of the archives. Policies, it was pointed out, could vary when dealing with different subjects. For example, if an archives collected records from a number of ethnic groups, the documentary goals for each group might vary, as would the existing information regarding the group. This being the case, different documentary goals might exist for different groups, which would be reflected in differing weights. If Italian material was top-heavy in terms of senior officers of fraternal organizations, collecting their records might be de-emphasized, lowering the weighted value of elements like position in organization. If material about religious practices within the Polish National Church were scarce, elements addressing this subject could be weighted more heavily. Establishing one set of weights for all institutional selection decisions fails to represent the complex interplay of collecting activity that can go on in an institution.

Developing a better way to establish accurate weighting numbers is important. Weights represent the intersection of record evaluation and institutional policy. Understanding what occurs at that junction is critical to understanding different selection practices in different archives. Developing this understanding, and accurate numbers to accompany it, will not be easy. There is no mathematical way to assign weights so that the numbers accurately reflect an archives' goals and policies. Archivists' ability to assign weights will develop through experience. The more archivists try to convert goals into numbers the more accurate the conversion will become. Pragmatic, practical efforts are the only way to eventually establish mathematically accurate weights, which will, in turn, help regularize and explain why particular selection decisions are made.

Modifying Thresholds and Kickers

Modifications could also be made in the way thresholds and kickers are applied. As they were originally conceived, thresholds applied only to scale scores equal to or greater than the threshold value. Threshold values defined the smallest allowable value for a scale score. This one-sided notion was inaccurate. In some cases an element became of concern only when it received a very low score. For example, the credibility scale ran from zero, totally incredible, to five, totally credible. Since almost all records received a five, this score was meaningless but nevertheless was included in each module calculation. Establishing a threshold value that disallowed credibility unless the scale value was one or less would have eliminated a common source of score inflation. Thresholds were useful at both the upper and the lower ends of the element scales.

Kickers also were conceived of in a one-sided way that was inaccurate. As originally designed kickers allowed archivists to automatically preserve records. It was noted, however, that there are times when the decision to discard records is made as quickly as the decision to save documents. An illegible record is just that and therefore will be destroyed.[15] Kickers, therefore, should be able to represent either extreme situation, booting a collection into or out of an archives.

The primary usefulness of kickers and thresholds, however, is in a mathematical methodology designed to predict selection decisions, rather than in one that systematizes and explains the decision. Therefore kickers and thresholds could be left out of a nonpredictive system without significant harm. That deletion, in fact, might aid the methodology's effectiveness since it would simplify the system. Although some form of final calculation would be of systematizing value, the current lack of a theoretical framework suggests that such a calculation should be excluded at this time.

Quantifying the selection decision-making process, even for communicative purposes, is a difficult task. It requires both an understanding of how selection decisions are reached and the development of numerical tools accurately reflecting this process. Both are difficult challenges but the effort to accomplish them is important because it will clarify the process of archival selection, and quantification itself is useful as a practical archival tool. It also resolves theoretical problems. Furthermore, the existence of an accurate quantification tool for selection would help define archivists' image among nonarchivists. Selection standards and quantification methods would not only demonstrate the unique judgments which archivists claim fall within their sphere of professional responsibilities, but would help to define the profession as well. For all these reasons the effort to quantify selection decisions should be continued.

QUANTIFICATION: CONCLUSION

It will be many years before archivists can develop a mathematical or computerized system that will duplicate the judgment of expert archival selection evaluators. Mathematical systems for selection nevertheless offer archivists important advantages that justify their continuing development and use. Numbers are a powerful rationalizing tool. Using numbers helps archivists standardize judgments about records. Furthermore, numbers help communicate those judgments between archivists for discussion and debate. Finally, numbers systematize reporting processes.

Beyond rationalization, developing numerical record evaluation systems forces archivists to think about and develop an understanding of the most challenging problems in selection. Both inductive and deductive logic can be fruitfully applied to the search for a better understanding of selection. Because numerical selection systems help rationalize archival judgment while allowing archivists to better understand that judgment, it is an extremely beneficial process for archivists to employ.

INSTITUTIONAL DIFFERENCES: INTRODUCTION

Archivists have often approached selection with a subconscious sense that its principles and methodology were universal. Although

Theodore Schellenberg was careful to note that his appraisal guidelines were explicitly drafted with federal records in mind, his guidelines were widely applied by institutional archivists and quickly became the standard when appraising institutional records. The Society of American Archivists' first published appraisal manual, written by Maynard Brichford, made little or no distinction regarding institutional differences in how selection should be undertaken. Subsequent authors, including Boles and Young, also supported the subconscious premise that there was a "right way" to appraise. Although Boles and Young allowed for the importance of institutional collecting policies on selection, they did not develop the implications of that statement.

Relative Differences By Institutional Type

When the *ranking of selection* elements used in this study were grouped by the type of archival institution in which participating archivists worked, institutional differences were suggested. These differences were most clear in the *information* and *implications* modules, which will be discussed in turn.

TABLE 5-2. Value-of-Information Module, Rank Order of Collapsed Elements by Institutional Type (*indicates identical rank)[16]

College & University	State Archives	Church Archives	Manuscript Repository	Average
1 Functional (3.89)	RM (3.84)	Functional (2.56)	Users (2.34)	Functional (2.92)
2 Intellectual Duplication (3.56)	Functional (3.22)	Use Limits (2.22)	Content* (2.33)	RM (2.80)
3 RM (3.00)	Users (3.00)	Users (2.00)	Intellectual Duplication* (2.33)	Users (2.58)
4 Content (2.78)	Intellectual Duplication (2.67)	RM (1.83)	Physical Duplication* (2.33)	Intellectual Duplication (2.51)
5 Physical Duplication (2.77)	Physical Duplication (2.55)	Content* (1.78)	RM (2.16)	Physical Duplication (2.44)
6 Users (2.67)	Use Limits (2.33)	Intellectual Duplication* (1.78)	Functional (2.11)	Content (2.26)
7 Use Limits (2.11)	Content (2.11)	Physical Duplication* (1.78)	Use Limits (1.89)	Use Limits (2.14)

The numbers and rankings found in Table 1 need to be approached with skepticism. The overall sample size is too small to be statistically valid and the subpopulation sizes (n) are as small as two. The table is provocative in what it hints at, but in no way conclusive in its results.

Despite the table's obvious limitations it does hint at two far-reaching conclusions. First, it suggests that the hypothesis that the *elements of information* evaluation is of unequal value is correct. Second, the table suggests that the importance of the elements is partly determined by the type of archival institution using them. This conclusion resurrects the classic distinction between archives and manuscript repositories, and more subtly suggests that there are distinctions between types of institutional archives.

In looking at the average ranking of the seven collapsed elements, it seems that archivists evaluate information using intellectual elements that are organized by difficulty of implementation. With a knowledge of institutional history, it is relatively easy to apply the elements in functional analysis. Similarly, implementing record management criteria is fairly simple once the institution's legal and administrative needs are defined. In principle, users are also fairly easy to consult, since they present themselves daily at the archives' door. Intellectual and physical duplication, however, are more difficult issues to deal with since determining duplication requires a detailed knowledge of both the physical universe of documentation and the intellectual character of that documentation. Content is a particularly difficult problem since it can involve detailed, time-consuming analysis of the records being evaluated. The bottom ranking of easily determined use limits does not neatly fit into the idea that archivists rank evaluative elements in order of their ease of use. However, use limits may have been considered so trivial by archivists participating in the study that they were not seriously considered when information was evaluated.

Ease of implementation may be another way of saying that archivists generally select the least expensive means of evaluating information. Archivists have long complained that their institutions are underfunded and understaffed. This budgetary reality, labelled by others as the archival cycle of poverty, limits archivists' options and may shape how archivists approach selection.[17]

Equal in importance to the distinction archivists make between elements is the distinction different types of archival institutions seem to make between the elements. Historically, the archival community drew a sharp line between *archivists*, those members of the profession who oversaw institutional records, and *manuscript curators*, those members of the profession whose primary responsibility involved collecting papers from personal owners. Over the past decade archivists have increasingly come to discuss the one world of archives and stress similarities in the profession. Distinctions between archivists and curators have been minimized or dismissed.

Without denying the existence of professional similarities, the table suggests that there also remain important differences in how archivists approach the evaluation of information. The most obvious difference is between institutional archivists and archivists involved in the collection of privately owned historical material. Manuscript archivists tended to focus on users and content-related criteria, whereas institutional archivists tended to focus on functional criteria. The different approaches of the two types of archivists can be explained by generalizing from their archival missions. Institutional archivists' primary mission is usually to document their institution, and therefore functional analysis is a very powerful tool in fulfilling their mandate. Understanding what the institution's primary functions and activities were, who made fundamental decisions about institutional functions and activities, and what records document those functions and activities is a productive way to document an institution. Manuscript archivists, however, are usually charged to document a subject. Although functional analysis can be of some help in determining whether records document a subject, ultimately the only way to truly know if the records relate to the subject is to examine their content.

Initially, one might think that the costs of information evaluation to the archives would lead to a certain similarity in approach between institutional archivists and manuscript curators. Costs, however, are relative to the volume of material examined. Where state archivists may literally have to evaluate millions of feet of records each year, manuscript curators may have to examine only a few hundred feet of material annually. Reducing the size of the material under consideration facilitates a more detailed evaluation of the material.

The table also indicates that institutional archives are more varied than the simple archivist-curator dichotomy suggests. Among institutional archives there are differences in approach to information evaluation which are most likely based on the relative usefulness of the elements in a specific environment. For example, state archivists working in the legalistic setting of governmental bureaucracy strongly rely on records management to evaluate records. An emphasis on public law, civil service regulation, and accountability to citizens creates an atmosphere in which bureaucrats accept the regulatory character of a record schedule. Academic archivists, on the other hand, rely far more on functional analysis than on records management. Records scheduling on college campuses often run afoul of an environment that emphasizes intellectual freedom and enshrines independence through mechanisms such as tenure. Faculty often have little time for "mindless bureaucratic regulations" such as record schedules. College administrators, often facing this independent attitude on a variety of fronts, are usually unwilling to invest their limited capital in fights over "mere records." Therefore, rather than relying on systematic record scheduling as their primary means of selecting archival records, college archivists rely first on functional analysis to determine the records they wish to acquire.[18]

Another way to look at the data in Table 2 is to ask what the range is between the highest and lowest ranked elements. This measure is a primitive way to measure if, and how much, archivists distinguish between the various elements used to evaluate information. On a one-to-four scale the average range was 0.76. Sharp differences, however, emerged when looking at types of archives. College and university archives showed a range of 1.78, state archives a nearly identical range of 1.73, church archives an almost normative 0.78, and manuscript archives an abnormally low range of 0.45. What these ranges suggests is that the rank order of elements is of more importance in some archives than others. College and university, as well as state archivists, have clear preferences for the way they approach the evaluation of information. Manuscript archivists, on the other hand, tend to draw extensively on virtually the whole range of evaluative criteria. This finding may be a result of the quantity of information that must be evaluated. Archivists with fewer records to consider have the luxury of looking at the information in those records with a larger number of evaluative tools. Nevertheless, it is of interest that archivists in certain types of archives have a clear preference when employing information evaluating criteria.

TABLE 5-3. Implications-of-the-Selection Decision Module, Rank Order of Elements

College & University	State	Church	Manuscript	Average
1 Authority (3.67)	Third Party (2.66)	Authority (1.66)	Information (2.33)	Authority (2.33)
2 Source (3.50)	Agreement (2.50)	Costs (1.66)	Costs (2.00)	Source (2.17)
3 Third Party (2.99)	Authority (2.33)	Information (1.33)	Authority (1.66)	Third Party (2.12)
4 Agreement (2.83)	Source (2.17)	Source (1.33)	Source (1.66)	Information (2.08)
5 Information (2.66)	Costs (2.00)	Third Party (1.33)	Agreement (1.50)	Agreement (1.96)
6 Costs (2.00)	Information (2.00)	Agreement (1.00)	Third Party (1.50)	Costs (1.92)

The limitations cited for Table 1 regarding the validity of the table also apply to Table 2. Because the elements of the *implications* module were poorly conceived, results drawn from Table 3 are even more suspect than those of Table 2. Overall, however, Table 3 supports the general propositions suggested by Table 2, that there is a difference between manuscript and institutional archivists and that there are also differences among institutional archivists.

Table 3 lends itself to only a few additional conclusions. The first is the markedly political character of college and university archives and state archives. These two groups of archivists displayed far more concern about the implications of their actions then either their religious or their manuscript colleagues. Second, the priority given by manuscript curators to internal policy concerns rather than external concerns is unique. Neither observation lends itself to a simple explanation. It is possible that the study groups were not representative of these attitudes.

INSTITUTIONAL DIFFERENCES: CONCLUSIONS

This study brings to light two basic points regarding institutional differences. First, archival institutions differ in the way record evaluative elements are applied to selection. There is no "one right way," to select records. Rather, selection is governed by institutional policy, as well as the realities imposed by the number of staff available for record evaluation and the quantity of records in need of examination. Second, the variability between institutions is not random. Instead, similar institutions will likely adopt similar evaluative approaches towards records. The greatest differences in evaluative approaches will be seen between institutions with obviously different missions. As a practical matter, this observation resurrects the seemingly dormant distinction once made between archivists and manuscript curators.

Endnotes

1. Sociologists refer to the process of converting abstractions into meaningful questions as *operationalization*. Operationalization is a difficult task since a poorly phrased or misworded question may not solicit responses relevant to the abstraction being tested.

2. Barbara Reed, "Acquisition and Appraisal", in Ann Pederson, ed., *Keeping Archives* (Sydney: Australian Society of Archives, 1987): 96. Reed recommends the use of appraisal checklists and notes that they may "...require a relative weighting to be completed for each criteria." Unfortunately she does not specify how Australian archivists accomplish this task. Charles H. Kepner and Benjamin B. Tregoe, *The New Rational Manager* (Princeton: Kepner-Tregoe, Inc., 1981): 93-98, discuss a similar

system of weighted score values which they recommend as a general approach to aid managers in making decisions.

3. Module 1 was unique because elements 17, 18, and 19 were subtracted from, not added to, the module score.

4. Ratio scores have been rounded to the nearest decimal and the ratio calculation is expressed in the form "Information + Implications/Costs" or "Information/Costs + Implications" depending upon whether implications were seen as positive or negative.

5. The collections information module score rankings were: 1. Bloom Township Road Records, 216; 2. Bloom Township School Fund Accounts, 201; 3. BGSU Personnel Files, 195; 3. Pauli Literary Documents, 195; 5. Pauli Printed, 184; 6. Pauli Correspondence, 179; 7. Toledo Symphony, 178; 8. Hill/Morgan Papers, 170; 9. BGSU Treasurer's Subject File, 148; 10. Bloom Township Chattel Mortgages, 145; 11. BGSU History Dept. Chairman's Correspondence, 116.

6. The collections combined information and implication module score ranks were: 1. Bloom Township Road Records, 247; 2. BGSU Personnel Files, 233; 3. Bloom Township School Fund Accounts, 232; 4. Pauli Literary Documents, 197; 5. Toledo Symphony, 196; 6. Pauli Printed Material, 186; 7. Pauli Correspondence, 181; 8. Bloom Township Chattel Mortgages, 176; 9. Hill/Morgan Papers, 172; 9. BGSU Treasurer's Subject File, 172; 11. BGSU History Dept. Chairman's Correspondence, 142.

7. I am indebted to Margaret Hedstrom for her thoughtful comments regarding the issues involved in developing a mathematical methodology. An alternate approach to developing an expert system would be to investigate "fuzzy logic" expert systems. The National Archives and Records Administration has funded research into this area by Avra Michelson. The fuzzy logic solution to the problem is likely to be a more profitable way to approach this problem, but it would still require significant intellectual work to develop the rules-of-thumb that a computer would use in conducting selection evaluations.

8. Glynn Harman, "Toward Expert Inquiry Systems", *Reference Librarian* 18 (Summer 1987): 96.

9. Characteristics listed in the matrix include age/scarcity, record function, utility, credibility, continuing administrative value, continuing financial value, continuing legal value, evidential characteristics, informational characteristics, research potential, relationship to other records, processing costs, preservation costs, search costs, and storage costs/volume. This matrix was distributed to Mellon Fellows at the University of Michigan's Bentley Library by Sidney McAlpern in 1982. In many ways it influenced this study of selection.

10. For more information regarding these projects see Michael Stephen Hindus, Theodore M. Hammett, and Barbara M. Hobson, *The Files of the Massachusetts Superior Court, 1859-1959: An Analysis and a Plan for Action* (Boston: G.K. Hall & Co., 1979): 59-61, and James Gregory Bradsher, "Researchers, Archivists, and the Access Challenge of the FBI Records in the National Archives," *Midwestern Archivist* 9 (1986): 95-110.

11. A copy of this form is in the possession of Julia Marks Young.

12. Paul K. Richard to Julia Marks Young, May 10, 1988 and attachments.

13. John Rutledge and Luke Swindler, "The Selection Decision: Defining Criteria and Establishing Priorities," *College & Research Libraries* 48 (March 1987): 129-130. I am indebted to Leonard Coombs for bringing this article to my attention.

14. Using numbers in this way is a relatively common management technique. See, for example, Charles H. Kepner and Benjamin B. Tregoe, *The New Rational Manager* (Princeton: Kepner-Tregoe, Inc., 1981): 92-137.

15. These kinds of concerns are most pronounced when dealing with computerized records. See, for example, Harold Naugler, *The Archival Appraisal of Machine-Readable Records: A RAMP Study with Guidelines* (Paris: General Information Programme and UNISIST, United Nations Educational Scientific and Cultural Organization, 1984): 57-58.

16. Asterisks indicate elements with identical average weights. Elements with identical weights are listed alphabetically in the table.

17. Edwin C. Bridges, "Consultant Report: State Government Records Programs," in Lisa B. Weber, ed., *Documenting America: Assessing the Condition of Historical Records in the States* (Atlanta: National Association of State Archives and Records Managers, 1984): 1. If this conclusion is true it has profound implications for other areas of archival work. Efforts to improve and standardize descriptive practices that include expensive "frills" like authority controls may, for example, run afoul of this "do it cheap" attitude.

18. The characterizations of the government and the academic environment given here are stereotypical. Government agencies can treat intellectual issues such as intellectual freedom in a sensitive manner, while college administrators can mindlessly enforce legalistic rules regardless of the impact.

6

Conclusions

In the course of this study a large number of findings have been reported and many selection possibilities and ideas have been explored. Many of the questions that remain are about the implications of these findings. Knowing the results of this study, how can the archival community use this knowledge to shape the selection of historical records in the late twentieth century? Knowing what archivists now know, what additional research should be undertaken?

The findings and discussion in *Archival Appraisal* suggest four areas of concern regarding the selection of information for long term retention. First, the study points to the critical importance to archivists of further developing their record selection methodology. Second, the findings and discussion presented here indicate the fundamental role of selection policy in determining which information is to be retained by an archives. Third, the report highlights the importance of the information environment and general policy context in which selection decisions are made. The fourth and last concern does not directly address a selection question, but rather takes the issues raised here about selection and fits them into the overall conceptual framework of archivists. Each of these concerns is a complex topic with significant implications.

RECORD SELECTION METHODOLOGY

Archivists have not created a well-defined methodology to govern selection. This failure has created a situation in which archivists possess a variety of selection tools and policies, but no clear sense about when particular tools are applied, how the tools interrelate, or how policy and tools should interact. Because of this lack of clarity, archivists' discussions of selection are often muddy. Sometimes, the same ideas are employed to try to explain the importance of vast quantities of records as well as the decision to retain an individual item. On other occasions there seems to be little or no connection between how archivists talk about the bulk of records and how archivists evaluate individual items.

The problem faced by archivists is similar to that faced by economists who must explain both broad trends in the economy and individual preferences in the grocery store. In order to describe both national agribusiness trends and why a shopper bought an apple rather than a pear, economists have developed sets of distinct, yet interrelated tools that apply to economic decisions made at different levels. Cast in its broadest terms, these are the instruments of macro and micro economics. Archivists need to realize that they have a similar need to explain both broad social documentation goals and the selection of specific records for archival preservation. The selection elements discussed in this report represent the micro-level tools used by archivists to accomplish the selection of specific records.

Specific selection elements are micro-level tools that have a fundamental impact upon the shape of archival information. Although they must be linked to policies and other macro-level concerns in order to be used intelligently, the relationship is not a one-sided, hierarchical structure in which policy creates marching orders to be implemented by archivists using micro-level elements. The capabilities and limitations of micro-level selection tools define the archivist's ability to successfully and fully implement policy decisions. An archival repository must have statements such as a collecting policy. It may prove useful for individual institutions or coalitions of archives to attempt to more systematically preserve information through the use of documentation strategies. But these policy documents, critical though they are, cannot be systematically implemented unless they rest upon an appropriate body of micro-level selection tools. Tools enable policy, policy does not enable tools.

Recognizing their critical importance, what can we say about the tools used by archivists to select information for long term retention? At one level, this study reveals that the archival community is approaching a common set of definitions regarding many of the various elements of selection. In the *value of information* module some problems remain, but they appear amenable to either logical solution or to the imposition of an arbitrary but standard interpretation. This study establishes logical definitions for many elements in the *value of information* module that may prove of enduring usefulness. It also points to the possibilities in establishing arbitrary definitions of other elements in the hope that by doing so, other archivists will initiate a discussion from which a consensus will shortly emerge. Definitions in the *costs* module appear relatively straightforward, and with the exception of the reference area, offer little difficulty. Within the implications module definitions may be premature. As the discussion of this module points out, the archival understanding of how it fits in with the other parts of selection is so preliminary that establishing a widely accepted intellectual framework and carefully delineating the elements in that framework is premature.

Applying Selection Tools Consistently

Although the archival community is approaching a common definition of selection tools, the same community has not developed a consistent method to apply these tools. Archivists have, in fact, sometimes resisted consistent selection procedures. In part, this may be based on a misreading of Theodore Schellenberg, whose endorsement of "diverse judgments" in selection has sometimes been interpreted as absolute license. Schellenberg's diverse judgments, however, were implicitly framed by institutional policy, through which, "Archivists of different archival institutions may ... use different criteria in evaluating similar types of records, for what is valuable to one archival institution may be valueless to another."[1]

The development of a consistent selection methodology will likely involve continuing work in two areas. First, the use of some kind of numbers will probably continue, in an effort to better express the exact nature and strength of an archivist's evaluation of records. Second, the sociological and psychological literature on decision making may serve as a springboard for understanding and eliminating hidden biases in the process by which records are selected for archival retention.

Developing Successful Formulas

For the reasons already suggested, numbers have a value in helping clarify the reasons why particular records are selected for archival retention and applying those reasons in a consistent and evenhanded manner. The specific formulas used in this study were an unsuccessful attempt to create a wide-ranging quantification scheme for selection. Even without the formulas, however, the improved communication that the use of numbers allows between archivists making selection decisions indicates it will have a continuing value. Any tool that allows archivists to speak to one another in a more precise way about selection is worth pursuing. In the long run an expert system for selection that is based on fuzzy logic, such as that being explored by the National Archives, may incorporate the use of numbers to help clarify the nature of the material that the system is being asked to evaluate.

The development of an expert selection system, however, requires that archivists define the elements of selection, develop rules-of-thumb to relate the elements one to another, and that they understand any hidden prejudices or biases implicit in the selection criteria. *Archival Appraisal* has addressed the question of definitions at great length here. The rules-of-thumb used in selection may begin to emerge from discussions held at the National Archives. However, the last area, hidden biases, is almost never discussed. The findings of this study, however, suggest that there are biases in archival selection criteria.

When archivists' preferences for specific selection elements are placed in the order given them by the participants in this study, it is clear that institutional archivists in particular use various record characteristics as substitutes for examining the records' content. The quantity of modern records makes it difficult or impossible for archivists to examine documents to determine content. A logical alternative to reading documents is to use specific record characteristics, such as the hierarchical position in a bureaucracy of the records' creator, or the creator's activities, as a substitute for content analysis. Logical as the alternative is, it also suggests the possibility of bias.

To exemplify this point, consider the impact of Schellenberg's evidential values on the documentation of America's nonelite groups. Archivists have long complained that the archival record is top-heavy in records created by society's elite, and impoverished regarding society's less fortunate. Archivists have tended to assume this is because not enough archival attention has been paid to the nonelite groups. But an archival selection method that relies heavily on elements such as *position in hierarchy* and *unit activities* will likely always be disproportionately focused on the elite members of society who occupy important offices. Even when evidential values are specifically aimed at nonelite groups, such as the so-called new immigrants of the late nineteenth and early twentieth centuries, the criteria has the disturbing result of documenting the nonelite's elite; that is, of selecting records created by an immigrant group's leaders, rather than by immigrants. The portrait painted of immigrant life by a Polish National Alliance leader in 1910 is as potentially skewed as the presentation of welfare statistics by the administrator of a state's Social Services agency. Neither person experiences the world from the bottom up.

Although it is true that Schellenberg balanced evidential values with informational concerns, in point of fact, most institutional archivists find it far easier to select documents based on evidential rather than informational criteria. The very nature of evidential values creates a structural bias towards the documentation of elites. If the structural bias of evidential values is clear, it is likely that other selection criteria also contain more subtle biases. The potential structural bias of selection elements is an important area for future archival research and discussion.

Drawing on Other Disciplines

The sociological and psychological literature on decision making may also be central to the better use of archival selection tools. No matter how careful and thorough archivists are, selection inevitably involves risks. Understanding how people behave when they make risky decisions, how they edit, evaluate, display data, and frame both questions and solutions all has a direct and significant impact on how archivists select information.[2]

Realizing the importance of various related fields' literature to the archival community is not to suggest that all archivists should become experts in sociology, psychology, or statistics. Perhaps because archivists have often argued that the practice of their profession requires a broad general knowledge, the discovery of new wisdom may unwisely tempt them to become experts in that field. Life is too short to become a good archivist, sociologist, psychologist, and statistician. But a small group of research-oriented archivists must explore the literature in these and other disciplines, extract from it information of value to archivists, and report their findings back to the archival community. All archivists cannot take the time to read and ponder the literature of related disciplines. Some archivists, however, *must* do so.

THE ROLE OF SELECTION POLICY

An understanding of micro-level selection tools and techniques can be informed by other professions and would benefit from a careful consideration of the biases implicit in those tools. Quantification may help archivists discuss the use of such tools more precisely. However, archivists' concern regarding micro-level tools should not obscure the importance of this study's second major point: the importance of policy in all selection decisions. Archival selection policies, more commonly labeled as mission statements and collecting policies, represent the macro-level tools that an archivist employs in selecting records.

Selection policies and documentary goals are critical archival policies that define the objectives and limits of an archival repository. The micro-level elements of selection can be used meaningfully only in the context of institutional policies. Micro-level tools identify characteristics and features of given records. Institutional policy answers the question of whether or not the material possessing certain characteristics and features belongs in a particular archives. If beauty is in the eye of the beholder, so too is historical value in the eye of the archivist, who must discern it in light of the mission and collecting policy of his or her repository.

To make the same point another way, it is relatively easy to look out at the information available about American society and conclude that certain aspects of American culture are poorly documented. The birth of many archival institutions—for example, the Immigration History Research Center at the University of Minnesota—resulted from just such observations regarding immigrant history. It is more difficult to take such an observation and translate it into a clearly focused archival collecting policy.

Recognizing that immigration is undocumented is not the same as stating how it should be documented. What immigrant groups are most important to document? What portion or portions of the immigrant experience is most significant? Does the domain of immigrant studies include not only the lives and institutions of the immigrants themselves but also the lives and institutions of the immigrants' children and grandchildren? Defining boundaries—that is, establishing policy—which answer these and many similar questions is a difficult and time-consuming task. It is, however, a task that may be done. After careful thought or lucky happenstance boundaries are drawn. A focus on certain immigrant groups is established. Particular aspects of the immigrant experience are selected for study. Limits are set in place.

This process of policy establishment is the same among institutional archivists as it is in the more subject-oriented world of manuscript archivists. Institutional archivists frequently argue that their mandate is to document the bureaucracy which employs them, and therefore they do not need a collecting policy. The law, executive order, or corporate authorization that establishes their mandate defines an institutional archivist's record retention goals. In point of fact, however, institutional archivists make a large number of collecting choices. Which offices in the institution are most important? What portion or portions of the institution's activities are most significant? Does every activity in all parts of a far-flung institutional structure need to be fully and completely documented, or is there some logical way to draw boundaries which exclude or severely limit the amount of information retained about certain aspects of the institution?

These questions are implicit in Theodore Schellenberg's long-used appraisal methods. For example, Schellenberg's concept of a documentary pyramid in which archivists should most concern themselves with records created by the administrators at the pyramid's apex, has clear collecting implications. Schellenberg's dismissal of housekeeping records as of minimal importance also has clear implications for the way an institutional archives will document the day-to-day activities of the organization.[3] After invoking Schellenberg for almost 40 years, many institutional archivists have forgotten that much of Schellenberg's decision making criteria involve the implementation of archival choices within the framework of federal records, not simply a legal mandate. Making these choices should be just as hard for institutional archivists as establishing collecting policy is for manuscript archivists. The choices that the institutional archivist makes are the de facto collecting policies of the archives.

Questions about collecting policy, while difficult, are manageable. Within institutions a focus on certain offices will emerge. As time passes it will become clear that particular aspects of the institution's history deserve to be better documented. Over time, boundaries regarding minimum documentation standards for the entire institution will be drawn or areas of the institution that the archives considers of no importance will be excluded. All archivists slowly develop collecting policy. The difference between a consciously managed archives and one that grows haphazardly is based primarily on the explicitness with which collecting policies are developed. Consciously managed policies develop explicit selection policies. Less organized archives lack clearly stated policies and in their place, rely on individual archivists' knowledge of their own past decisions, the physical presence of past accessions, and an oral tradition regarding the institution's past actions. It should come as no surprise that the results of this study suggest that conscious selection policymaking is preferable to the more serendipitous alternative employed by many archivists.

Although the need for and structure of collecting policy development is likely to be common in a wide variety of archives, the final result will remain a unique institutional policy. This study has repeatedly made the point that there is no one set of policies, objectives, or goals that can be applied in all archival settings. Although all archives share in a general cultural objective of documenting society, the exact mission and responsibility of each archival institution is locally determined. It is possible to lament some of the consequences of this decentralized policymaking pattern, but without major and highly unlikely changes in the structure of the American archival community, it is the framework in which American archivists will develop future collecting policies.

As a consequence of this framework, each archives sets its own agenda. It is at liberty to cooperate, or not cooperate, with institutions sharing a similar agenda or geographic location. While a growing sense of professionalism may limit outright competition, as well as exert a force toward cooperation, ultimately it is the wishes of those who fund archival institutions that will be followed, rather than any professional imperative generated by archivists themselves. So long as archival sources of funding and accountability are diverse, archival policies and goals will remain pluralistic. The common need for collecting policies should not be misinterpreted as an engine driving archives towards a single, common collecting policy.

THE GENERAL ENVIRONMENT OF SELECTION POLICY

A third major area of concern in this report has been the role of the environment within the selection process. There are two environments that affect selection; the policy environment and the information environment.

Although specific selection policies are a critical and important part of any archives mission, archivists must remember the third basic issue raised by this study; that selection policy is only one of many institutional policies. Selection policy is so important that many archivists tend to consider it in isolation from other institutional goals and priorities. In fact, some archivists may resent and oppose the integration of selection policy with other institutional policies on the grounds that the process will somehow sully the purity of selection. "Other" concerns will lead to the bending or breaking of selection criteria in ways inimical to the long-term documentation objectives of the archives.

This argument implicitly presents selection policy as a fragile structure unable to assert itself against other policy considerations in an archival institution. Gathering documentation, however, is the core goal of an archives, and therefore the policy outlining the documentation objectives should be among the archive's most robust policy documents. If collecting policy is fragile, it is most likely because the archives' staff has not articulated the policy in a clear, forceful, and understandable manner. A policy that rests primarily upon individual interpretation is likely to be fragile. It lacks a consensus within the archives and among the archives' supporters. A clearly articulated and well supported selection policy should be a strong document. Even when the archives reports within a broader institutional framework, the centrality of collecting policy to the archives' mission should make it clear to everyone that only under extraordinary circumstances should collecting policy be made subordinate to other archival goals or the goals of the parent institution.

But extraordinary circumstances do occur, both in an archives and in an archives' parent institution. It is the recognition that selection policy is just one policy among many that makes it possible to logically discuss and reconcile the interaction of these various policies. The importance of selection policy can be defended against the importance of another policy with which it may be in conflict. In that sort of logical debate the centrality of collecting policy to the archives' mission can often be contrasted against other, lesser policy concerns. Logically, the lesser concerns will fall aside and leave selection policy intact. In those few cases when, in comparison to another goal, selection policy appears the lesser objective, it makes no institutional sense for the archivist to insist upon blind adherence to selection policy. Archival selection policies are not issued from on high nor carved in stone. They are an important part of overall institutional policies but they are only a part, a fact archivists must understand.

The Information Environment

Like the policy environment, the information environment surrounding selection is also of critical importance. The archival community is apparently developing a professional consensus that its limited resources should be focused on truly unique information. Without engaging in a long discussion about what truly unique information is, this focus on uniqueness has had two significant results. First, archivists have decided to cast their information net broadly and compare the information they find in their holdings against not only other archival material, but also material found in a variety of other sources, such as published items. Second, archivists have developed an interest in limiting the number of individually unique yet collectively similar documents that are the product of modern society. Typical examples of this phenomenon are welfare case files maintained in each of the fifty states or classroom teaching material for introductory courses taught in colleges and universities across America. Although this emerging consensus is generally wise, it contains limitations that must be acknowledged.

These limitations flow from the diversity in archival institution's sources of funding and accountability. In many cases, these sources require that individual archives adopt collectively redundant missions. The State of New York mandates its archives to carry on certain basic activities, as do the states of Illinois and Alabama. Although archivists in these states have significant freedom of action, fulfilling the basic documentary mandate of each state's government will likely involve the retention of essentially identical records in each state's archives. New York is not likely to throw away its governor's records on the grounds that a similar set of records documenting approximately the same issues has been preserved in Illinois.

College and university archives face a similar dilemma. Bowling Green State University mandates that its university archives preserve certain documentation, as do the Massachusetts Institute of Technology and New York University. MIT is unlikely to schedule the records of its president for elimination on the grounds that another prestigious private school, such as New York University, has preserved the parallel files created by that school's president. Although there is room for cooperation in many selection areas, the essential redundancy of many archives' basic mission creates a situation where local responsibilities mandate the retention of information which is very similar or redundant on the national level. The continuing importance of local concerns is a fundamental reality that archivists need to accept and incorporate into their future planning activities for cooperative documentation projects.

HOW ARCHIVISTS SEE THEMSELVES

The last set of questions that this report raises is about how its findings fit into the archival community's conception of itself. Addressing this question in its most sweeping terms, this report suggests that archival literature may have overstated the size and impact of the movement toward professional uniformity that emerged in the 1960s and 1970s. If one takes the literature seriously, over the past thirty years the distinctions that have separated those responsible for primary material have blurred to the point where it is possible to discuss "one world of archives." A typical example of how the literature has addressed this merging of professional skill is found in the writing of Richard Berner.

Berner conceptualizes archivists' professional roots in two distinct and disparate sources; the historic manuscripts tradition and the public archives tradition. In the United States, Berner believes the historic manuscripts tradition is rooted firmly in scholarly research and draws upon descriptive paradigms developed by librarians to make collections of once privately owned manuscripts available to researchers. In contrast, the public archives tradition draws upon notions of administrative responsibility and public accountability to apply group descriptive approaches to governmental or other bureaucratic records. In discussing the two traditions' evolution, Berner concludes that the archival community has slowly but consistently adopted the standards of the public archives tradition as the community's professional standard. The historic manuscripts tradition, Berner concludes, has entered into a twilight, although Berner notes that it is the long-lasting twilight of an arctic summer's night.[4]

This study reinforces the notion of continuing diversity within the archival community that Berner suggests with his metaphor of arctic twilight. The documentation of an apparent distinction between how institutional archivists and noninstitutional archivists approach the evaluation of information suggests that the one world of archives continues to contain significant discontinuities. In the late 1980s diversity and pluralistic approaches to selection continue to exist among archivists. Neither the ascendancy of one tradition nor the less radical idea of a synthesis of two archival traditions appears to have successfully created a consistent use of selection elements by archivists.

One obvious but controversial thesis explaining the use of selection criteria by archivists in this study is that classic archival thought about professional development has overstated the convergence of divergent traditions. The development of a common professional terminology, and certain common arrangement and descriptive practices suitable for coping with collections containing a large volume of records, have been misinterpreted to indicate a common approach to archival problems. This thesis would hold that despite many common professional characteristics, the archival community remains highly pluralistic.

The acceptance of a model that envisions the archival community as a permanently pluralistic entity would have profound impact on a variety of professional concerns. Two examples, regarding common descriptive standards and archival education, demonstrate the point. In the past several years, work toward a national archival descriptive system has been fueled by the successful implementation of the MARC-AMC computer format and the creation of large, national databases containing MARC-AMC formatted descriptions. Although technically successful, problems of intellectual access within MARC-AMC databases have led to additional work regarding intellectual descriptive standards. If a pluralistic archival model is accepted, successful development of intellectual standards for description becomes increasingly difficult, since a broad range of interests need to be accommodated. Similarly, archival education assumes a core of professional knowledge. A pluralistic archival community, however, would have a smaller base core of knowledge and a larger specific body of information. In one scenario, competing schools of archival education might develop, with each school slanting its instruction to serve the need of a particular archival constituency.

The differences discovered in this study between various types of institutional archivists, as well as differences between institutional and noninstitutional archivists, are not profound enough in and of themselves to justify claims that archivists do not share a common bond. However, the findings do suggest that the archival community may draw upon and continue to nourish a complex system of interacting pluralistic beliefs and attitudes. To make such a claim will disturb those archivists who believe professionalism is synonymous with uniformity, but it also suggests that the archival community, by being able to draw upon a pluralistic base of knowledge and beliefs, has an improved potential to develop effective answers to the changes in information storage and processing that await us in the future.

Endnotes

1. T. R. Schellenberg, *The Appraisal of Modern Public Records*, 1956, reprinted in *A Modern Archives Reader: Basic Readings on Archival Theory and Practice*, Maygene F. Daniels and Timothy Walch, eds. (Washington D.C.: National Archives and Records Administration, 1984): 68.

It should also be noted that Schellenberg did not believe possible the kind of consistency in selection that this volume argues for.

2.   A starting point for those interested in questions of decision making would be Robin M. Hogarth, *Judgement and Choice* (2nd ed.) (New York: John Wiley & Sons, 1987).

3.   T.R. Schellenberg, *Modern Archives: Principles and Techniques* (Chicago: University of Chicago Press, 1956). Reprinted by Midway Editions, 1975, p. 143-144; 146.

4.   Richard C. Berner, *Archival Theory and Practice in the United States: A Historical Analysis* (Seattle: University of Washington Press, 1983). Reference to the HMT's "twilight" is on p. 73.

Bibliography

Alexander, Philip N. and Helen W. Samuels. "The Roots of 128: A Hypothetical Documentation Strategy." *American Archivist* 50 (1987): 518-531.

Anderson, Paul G. "Appraisal of the Papers of Biomedical Scientists and
Physicians for Medical Archives." *Bulletin of the Medical Library Association* 73 (October 1985): 338-344.

Aronsson, Patricia, "Appraisal of Twentieth-Century Congressional Collec-
tions." In *Archival Choices: Managing the Historical Record in an Age of
Abundance,* edited by Nancy Peace, 81-104. Lexington, MA: DC Heath
& Co., 1984.

Australian Archives. *Investigating the Value of Commonwealth Records: A
Self-Help Appraisal Handbook of Commonwealth Agencies.* Canberra:
Australian Government Publishing Service, 1987.

Bauer, G. Philip. "The Appraisal of Current and Recent Records." *The
National Archives Staff Information Circulars* 13 (June 1946): 1-22.

Benedict, Karen. "Invitation to a Bonfire: Reappraisal and Deaccessioning of
Records as Collection Management Tools in an Archives—A Reply to
Leonard Rapport." *American Archivist* 47 (Winter 1984): 43-49.

Benedon, William. *Records Management.* Englewood Cliffs, NJ: Prentice
Hall, 1969.

Blouin, Francis X., Jr. "An Agenda for the Appraisal of Business Records." In
*Archival Choices: Managing the Historical Record in an Age of Abun-
dance*, edited by Nancy E. Peace, 61-80. Lexington, MA: D.C. Heath &
Co., 1984.

———. "A New Perspective on the Appraisal of Business Records: A Review."
American Archivist 42 (July 1979): 312-320.

Boles, Frank. "Mix Two Parts Interest to One Part Information and
Appraise Until Done: Understanding Contemporary Record Selection
Processes." *American Archivist* 50 (Summer 1987): 356-68.

Boles, Frank, and Julia Marks Young. "Exploring the Black Box: The
Appraisal of University Administrative Records." *American Archivist* 48
(Spring 1985): 121-140.

Booms, Hans. "Society and the Formation of a Documentary Heritage:
Issues in the Appraisal of Archival Sources." *Archivaria* 24 (Summer
1987): 69-107.

Brichford, Maynard J. "Appraisal and Processing." In *College and University Archives: Selected Readings*, 8-17. Chicago: Society of American Archivists, 1979.

———. *Archives and Manuscripts: Appraisal and Accessioning*. Society of American Archivists Basic Manual Series. Chicago: Society of American Archivists, 1979.

———. *Scientific and Technological Documentation: Archival Evaluation and Processing of University Records Relating to Science and Technology*. Urbana-Champaign: University of Illinois, 1969.

———. "University Archives: Relationship with Faculty." In *College and University Archives: Selected Readings*, 31-37. Chicago: Society of American Archivists, 1979.

Brooks, Phillip C. "The Selection of Records for Preservation." *American Archivist* 3 (October 1940): 221-34.

Brown, C. "Deaccessioning for the Greater Good." *Wilson Library Bulletin* 61 (April 1987): 22-24.

Cameron, Ross J. "Appraisal Strategies for Machine-Readable Case Files." *Provenance* 1 (Spring 1983): 49-55.

Chestnut, Paul. "Appraising the Papers of State Legislators." *American Archivist* 48 (Spring 1985): 159-72.

Collingridge, J. H. "The Selection of Archives for Permanent Preservation." *Archivum* 6 (1956): 25-35.

Conference on the Research Use and Disposition of Senators' Papers, *Proceedings*. Edited by Richard A. Baker. Washington, D.C.: n.p., 1979.

Cook, Michael. *Archives Administration*. Folkstone, Kent, England: Dawson, 1977.

———. *Archives and the Computer*. London: Butterworths, 1980.

Cox, Richard, J. "A Documentation Case Strategy Case Study: Western New York." *American Archivist* 52 (Summer 1989): 192-200.

Cox, Richard J., and Helen W. Samuels. "The Archivist's First Responsibility: A Research Agenda to Improve the Identification and Retention of Records of Enduring Value." *American Archivist* 51 (Winter 1988): 28-42.

Cronenwett, Philip N. "Appraisal of Literary Manuscripts." In *Archival Choices: Managing the Historical Record in an Age of Abundance*, edited by Nancy E. Peace, 105-16. Lexington, MA: D.C. Heath & Co., 1984.

Daniels, Maygene F. "Records Appraisal and Disposition." In *Managing Archives and Archival Institutions*, edited by James Gregory Bradsher, 53-66. Chicago: University of Chicago Press, 1988.

Darter, Lewis J., Jr. "Records Appraisal: A Demanding Task." *Indian Archives* 19 (1969): 1-9.

Day, Deborah Cozort. "Appraisal Guidelines for Reprint Collections." *American Archivist* 48 (Winter 1985): 56-63.

Dojka, John, and Sheila Conneen. "Records Management as an Appraisal Tool in College and University Archives." In *Archival Choices: Managing the Historical Record in an Age of Abundance*, edited by Nancy E. Peace, 19-60. Lexington, MA: D.C. Heath & Co., 1984.

Dollar, Charles. "Appraising Machine-Readable Records." *American Archivist* 41 (October 1978): 423-30.

———. "Machine-Readable Records of the Federal Government and the National Archives." In *Archivists and Machine-Readable Records*, edited by Carolyn L. Geda, Erik W. Austin, and Francis X. Blouin, Jr., 79-88. Chicago: Society of American Archivists, 1980.

Dowler, Lawrence. "Deaccessioning Collections: A New Perspective on a Continuing Controversy." In *Archival Choices: Managing the Historical Record in an Age of Abundance*, edited by Nancy E. Peace, 117-32. Lexington, MA: D.C. Heath & Co., 1984.

Eckersley, Timothy. "The Selection of Recordings for Permanent Retention in the BBC Sound Archives." *Phonographic Bulletin* 9 (1974): 9-12.

Ehrenberg, Ralph E. "Aural and Graphic Archives and Manuscripts." *Drexel Library Quarterly* 11 (January 1975): 55-71.

Elliot, Clark. "Communications and Events in History: Toward a Theory for Documenting the Past." *American Archivist* 48 (Fall 1985): 357-368.

Elzy, Martin L. "Scholarship vs. Economy: Records Appraisal at the National Archives." *Prologue* 6 (Fall 1974): 183-188.

Endelman, Judith E. "Looking Backward to Plan for the Future: Collection Analysis for Manuscript Repositories." *American Archivist* 50 (Summer 1987): 340-55.

Evans, Max J. "The Invisible Hand: Creating a Practical Mechanism for Cooperative Appraisal." *Midwestern Archivist* 11 (1986): 7-13.

Fagerlund, Liisa. "Records Management as an Appraisal Tool?" *Proceedings of the Joint Meeting of the Association of British Columbia Archivists and the Northwest Archivists*, Victoria, B.C., April 23-25, 1981.

Falb, Susan Rosenfeld. "The Social Historian and Archival Appraisal." Organization of American Historians *Newsletter*, February 1984.

Fedders, John M. and Lauryn H. Gutterplan. "Document Retention and Destruction: Practical, Legal and Ethical Considerations." *Notre Dame Lawyer* 56 (October 1980): 7-64.

Fishbein, Meyer H. "Appraisal of Twentieth Century Records for Historical Use." *Illinois Libraries* 52 (February 1970): 154-62.

―――. "Appraising Information in Machine-Language Form." *American Archivist* 35 (January 1972): 35-43.

―――. "Reflections on Appraising Statistical Records." *American Archivist* 50 (Spring 1987): 226-34.

―――. "The 'Traditional' Archivist and the Appraisal of Machine-Readable Records." In *Archivists and Machine-Readable Records,* edited by Carolyn L. Geda, Erik W. Austin, and Francis X. Blouin, Jr., 56-61. Chicago: Society of American Archivists, 1980.

―――. "A Viewpoint on the Appraisal of National Records." *American Archivist* 33 (April 1970): 175-87.

Fogerty, James E. "Manuscript Collecting in Archival Networks." *Midwestern Archivist* 6 (1982): 130-41.

Fox, Michael J., and Kathleen A. McDonough. *Wisconsin Municipal Records Manual.* Madison: State Historical Society of Wisconsin, 1980.

Gallagher, Connell. "Problems of the Collection Development Archivist." *AB: Bookman's Weekly* 85 (March 19, 1990): 1225-1230.

Garrison, Ellen. "The Very Model of a Modern Major General: Documentation Strategy and the Center for Popular Music." *Provenance* (Fall 1989): 22-32.

Guptil, M. B. *Archival Appraisal of Records of International Organizations.* Paris: UNESCO, 1985.

Haas, Joan Krizack, Helen Willa Samuels, and Barbara Trippel Simmons. *Appraising Records of Contemporary Science and Technology: A Guide.* Cambridge, MA: n.p., 1985.

Haas, Richard L. "Collection Reappraisal: The Experience at the University of Cincinnati." *American Archivist* (Winter 1984): 51-54.

Hackman, Larry, and Joan Warner-Blewett. "The Documentation Strategy Process: A Model and a Case Study." *American Archivist* 50 (Winter 1987): 12-47.

Haller, Uli. "Appraisal in Context." *Provenance* 1 (Fall 1983): 65-71.

Ham, F. Gerald. "Archival Choices: Managing the Historical Record in an Age of Abundance." American Archivist 47 (Winter 1984): 11-22. Also in *Archival Choices: Managing the Historical Record in an Age of Abundance,* edited by Nancy E. Peace, 133-48. Lexington, MA: D.C. Heath & Co., 1984.

————. "The Archival Edge." *American Archivist* 38 (January 1975): 5-13.

————. "Archival Strategies for the Post-Custodial Era." *American Archivist* 44 (Summer 1981): 207-16.

Harrison, Helen P. *The Archival Appraisal of Sound Recordings and Related Material.* Paris: UNESCO, 1987.

Hays, Samuel P. "The Use of Archives for Historical Statistical Inquiry." *Prologue* 1 (Fall 1969): 7-15.

Hedstrom, Margaret. "New Appraisal Techniques: The Effect of Theory on Practice." *Provenance* 7 (Fall 1989): 1-21.

Henry, Linda J. "Collecting Policies of Special-Subject Repositories." *American Archivist* 33 (Winter 1980): 57-63.

Hindus, Michael Stephens, Theodore M. Hammett, and Barbara M. Hobson. *The Files of the Massachusetts Superior Court, 1859-1959: An Analysis and a Plan for Action.* Boston: G.K. Hall, 1979.

Honhart, Frederick L. "The Solicitation, Appraisal, and Acquisition of Faculty Papers." *College and Research Libraries* 44 (May 1983): 236-41.

Hower, Ralph M. "The Preservation of Business Records." *Bulletin of the Business Historical Society* 11 (October 1937): 37-83.

Hurley, F. Jack. "There's More Than Meets the Eye: Looking at Photographs Historically." Center for Southern Folklore *Newsletter* 3 (Winter 1981): 6-7.

Iacovino, Livia. "The Development of the Principles of Appraisal in the Public Sector and Their Application to Business Records." *Archives and Manuscripts* (Australia) 17 (November 1989): 197-218.

"Intrinsic Value in Archival Material." *Staff Information Papers* 21. Washington D.C.: National Archives and Records Service, (1982).

Janzen, Mary E. "Pruning the Groves of Academe: Appraisal, Arrangement, and Description of Faculty Papers." *Georgia Archives* 9 (Fall 1981): 31-42.

Jenkinson, Hilary. *A Manual of Archive Administration.* 1937. Reprint. London: Percy Lund, Humphries & Co., 1965.

————. "The Problem of Elimination in the Records of Public Departments." In *Government Information and the Research Worker,* edited by Ronald Stavely, 18-32. London: The Library Association, 1952.

Joint Committee on Archives of Science and Technology (JCAST). *Understanding Progress as Process: Documentation of the History of Post-War Science and Technology in the United States.* Edited by Clark A. Elliott, 1983.

Kahn, Herman. "Mr. Kahn's Comments." In "The Appraisal of Current and Recent Records," by G. Philip Bauer, 22-25. *The National Archives Staff Information Circulars* 13 (June 1946).

Kane, Lucille M. "A Guide to the Care and Administration of Manuscripts." *Bulletins of the American Association for State and Local History* 2 (September 1960): [327]-88.

Kesner, Richard. "Labor Union Grievance Records: An Appraisal Strategy." *Archivaria* 8 (Summer 1979): 102-14.

Klaassen, David. "The Provenance of Social Work Case Records: Implications for Archival Appraisal and Access." *Provenance* 1 (Spring 1983): 5-26.

Kowlowitz, Alan. "Archival Appraisal of Online Information Systems." *Archival Informatics Technical Reports* 2 (Fall 1988).

Kromnow, Ake. "The Appraisal of Contemporary Records." Eighth International Congress on Archives, Washington, D.C., 1976.

Kula, Sam. *The Archival Appraisal of Moving Images: A RAMP Study with Guidelines.* Paris: UNESCO, 1983.

Lamb, W. Kaye. "The Fine Art of Destruction." *In Essays in Memory of Sir Hilary Jenkinson,* edited by Albert E. J. Hollaender, 50-56. Chichester, Sussex, England: Moore and Tillyer, 1962.

Leahy, Emmett J. "The Reduction of Public Records." *American Archivist* 3 (January 1940): 13-38.

Leahy, Emmett J., and Christopher A. Cameron. *Modern Records Management.* McGraw-Hill, 1956.

Leary, W. H. *The Archival Appraisal of Photographs: A RAMP Study.* Paris: UNESCO, 1985.

Levine, David. "The Appraisal Policy of the Ohio State Archives." *American Archivist* 47 (Summer 1984): 291-93.

———. "Social Service Programs: Appraisal of State and Local Records." *Provenance* 1 (Spring 1983): 31-39.

Lewinson, Paul. "Towards Accessioning Standards-Research Records." *American Archivist* 23 (July 1960): 297-309.

Lovett, Robert W. "The Appraisal of Older Business Records." *American Archivist* 15 (April 1952): 231-39.

———. "Looking Around." *Harvard Business Review* 29 (March 1951): 127-39.

Lucas, Lydia. "Managing Congressional Papers: A Repository View." *American Archivist* 41 (July 1978): 275-80.

Lutzker, Michael A. "Max Weber and the Analysis of Modern Bureaucratic Organization: Notes Toward a Theory of Appraisal." *American Archivist* 45 (Spring 1982): 119-30.

Mamonov, V. M. "Work Experience of Archival Institutions in the Soviet Union on Selection of Documents and Organisation of State Archives Fonds." *Indian Archives* 35 (July-December 1986): 1-8.

Marks, Donald. "AACRAO's *Guide for Retention and Disposal of Student Records*: A Critical Review." *Midwestern Archivist* 8 (1983): 27-33.

McCree, Mary Lynn. "Good Sense and Good Judgement: Defining Collections and Collecting." *Drexel Library Quarterly* 11 (January 1975): 21-33.

Meissner, Dennis E. "The Evaluation of Modern Business Accounting Records." *Midwestern Archivist* 5 (1981): 75-100.

Mills, Thomas E. "Archival Considerations in the Management of Machine-Readable Records in New York State Government." In *Archivists and Machine-Readable Records*, edited by Carolyn L. Geda, Erik W. Austin, and Francis X. Blouin, Jr., 102-10. Chicago: Society of American Archivists, 1980.

Mitchell, Thornton W. "New Viewpoints on Establishing Permanent Values of State Archives." *American Archivist* 33 (April 1970): 163-74.

National Archives and Records Service. *Disposition of Federal Records.* Washington, D.C: National Archives and Records Service, 1981.

———. *General Records Schedules.* Washington, D.C. National Archives and Records Service, 1982.

———. *Records Disposition Procedures.* Washington, D.C. National Archives and Records Service, 1979.

———. Office of Federal Records Centers. *Federal Archives and Records Centers.* Washington, D.C.: National Archives and Records Service, 1979.

———. Task Force on Appraisal and Disposition of Federal Records. *Appraisal and Disposition Policies in NARS: A Report and Recommendations to the Archivist of the United States on Performance of the Appraisal and Disposition Functions in the National Archives and Records Service.* Washington D.C.: National Archives and Records Service, 1983.

Naugler, Harold. *The Archival Appraisal of Machine-Readable Records: A RAMP Study with Guidelines.* Paris: UNESCO, 1984.

———. "The Machine-Readable Archives Program at the Public Archives of Canada: The First Five Years." In *Archivists and Machine-Readable Records,* edited by Carolyn L. Geda, Erik W. Austin, and Francis X. Blouin, Jr., 67-78. Chicago: Society of American Archivists, 1980.

Noble, Richard. "Considerations for Evaluating Local History Photographs." *Picturescope* 31 (Spring 1984): 17-21.

Norton, Margaret Cross. *Norton on Archives: The Writings of Margaret Cross Norton on Archival and Records Management.* Edited by Thornton W. Mitchell. Carbondale, IL: Southern Illinois University Press, 1975.

Ohio Municipal Records Manual, Edited by David Levine. Columbus, OH: The Ohio Historical Society, 1981.

O'Shea, Michael F. "Classification, Retention, and Automation: A Case Study." *Records and Retrieval Report* 4 (June 1988): 1-15.

Peace, Nancy E. "Deciding What to Save: Fifty Years of Theory and Practice." In *Archival Choices: Managing the Historical Record in an Age of Abundance,* edited by Nancy E. Peace, 1-18. Lexington, MA: D.C. Heath & Co., 1984.

Phillips, Faye. "Developing Collecting Policies for Manuscript Collections." *American Archivist* 47 (Winter 1984): 30-42.

Pinkett, Harold T. "Identification of Records of Continuing Value." *Indian Archives* 16 (1965/1966): 54-61.

———. "Selective Preservation of General Correspondence." *American Archivist* 30 (January 1967): 33-43.

Quinn, Patrick J. "Academic Archivists and Their Current Practice: Some Modest Suggestions." *Georgia Archives* 10 (Fall 1982): 14-24.

Rapport, Leonard. "No Grandfather Clause: Reappraising Accessioned Records." *American Archivist* 44 (Spring 1981): 143-50.

———. "In the Valley of Decision: What To Do about the Multitude of Files of Quasi Cases." *American Archivist* 48 (Spring 1985): 173-189.

Reed, Barbara. "Acquisition and Appraisal." In *Keeping Archives,* edited by Ann Pederson, 73-114. Sydney: Australian Society of Archives, 1987.

Reed-Scott, Jutta. "Collection Management Strategies for Archivists." *American Archivist* 47 (Winter 1984): 23-29.

"Report of the Ad Hoc Committee on Manuscripts Set Up by the American Historical Association in December 1948." *American Archivist* 14 (July 1951): 229-40.

Ritzenthaler, Mary Lynn, Gerald J. Munoff, and Margery S. Long. *Archives and Manuscripts: Administration of Photographic Collections.* SAA Basic Manual Series. Chicago: Society of American Archivists, 1984.

Roper, Michael. "Machine-Readable Records and the Public Record Office." In *Archivists and Machine-Readable Records,* edited by Carolyn L. Geda, Erik W. Austin, and Francis X. Blouin, Jr., 89-101. Chicago: Society of American Archivists, 1980.

Santen, Vernon B. "Appraisal of Financial Records." *American Archivist* 32 (October 1969): 357-61.

Schellenberg, T. R. "The Appraisal of Modern Records." *Bulletins of the National Archives* 8. Washington, D.C., 1956.

———. *Modern Archives: Principles and Techniques.* Chicago: University of Chicago Press, 1956.

Schuursma, Rolf L. "Principles of Selection." *Phonographic Bulletin* 9 (1974): 7-8; and "Principles of Selection in Sound Archives." *Phonographic Bulletin* 11 (1975): 12-19.

Steinwall, Susan D. "Appraisal and the FBI Files Case: For Whom Do Archivists Retain Records?" *American Archivist* 49 (Winter 1986): 52-64.

Thompson, Gloria A. "From Profile to Policy: A Minnesota Historical Society Case Study in Collection Development." *Midwestern Archivist* 8 (1983): 29-39.

Yates, JoAnne. "Internal Communication Systems in American Business Structure: A Framework to Aid Appraisal." *American Archivist* 48 (Spring 1985): 141-158.

Index